A BIOGRAPHY OF THOMAS WOLFE

A BIOGRAPHY OF THOMAS WOLFE

By Neal F. Austin

ROGER BEACHAM · PUBLISHER

PERMISSIONS

ACKNOWLEDGMENTS

Every book is the product of many minds. Not all those who have helped with this book can be mentioned here.

But I am especially grateful to those publishers who permitted the use of quotations from books by and about Thomas Wolfe.

I also must express gratitude to the Pack Memorial Library of Asheville, North Carolina, for the use of its collection of material about Thomas Wolfe and for the photographs used throughout this book. Special thanks goes to Myra Champion of the library's staff, who guided me through the collection and shared her own knowledge with me. I am similarly indebted to William S. Powell of the Louis Round Wilson Library of the University of North Carolina.

Finally, my sincere thanks to Barbara Holman, whose careful reading of the manuscript resulted in a better book.

NEAL F. AUSTIN

High Point, North Carolina
October 1, 1967

For BETTY SHAW AUSTIN

It was bright August
when we met and talked of Tom.

A BIOGRAPHY OF THOMAS WOLFE

1

They saw him plunge to house and shop, they saw him bent above his marbles, they saw him mold in his great hands—with curse and howl and passionate devotion—the rich texture of his home.

Look Homeward, Angel

THE TALL STONE-CUTTER stood for a moment looking at the work he had just finished. His blue eyes were steady as he examined critically the flat planes, the delicately wrought wreath of flowers, the carefully excised letters. It was, he saw, a good piece of work—good enough to meet his high standards.

He laid his tools aside, and, taking off his long shop apron, he stepped back several paces to look at the stone again. No tombstone ever left W. O. Wolfe's shop without this careful inspection.

Satisfied with the stone, he turned his attention to his clothes. He flicked away a smudge of dust from the leg of his trousers and with a cloth wiped his black shoes. Even at work, Oliver Wolfe was always elegantly dressed.

He always wore a long alpaca coat, striped trousers, a gray vest, white shirt with a wing collar and perfectly knotted tie. His only concession to the dustiness of his work or to the heat of the shop was to replace his coat with the long apron when he worked.

He took a final look at the stone, then went into his cluttered office. Leaning over the desk, he rummaged through piles of papers. There were letters, receipts, statements, little booklets containing stock verses for tombstones, and small

4

samples of granite and marble all piled in confusion. He pawed through them with his big hands until he found his battered day-book. He made a brief notation in the book, closed it, and prepared to leave for the day.

Before he left the building, however, he paused to say good-night to Mr. Jeanneret, the Swiss watchmaker whose shop occupied a small railed-off corner of the building. There was a strong bond of understanding between these two dissimilar men. Their frequent arguments about politics usually ended with much shouting and raving from Oliver. Mr. Jeanneret accepted, even if he did not understand, the storm in the stone-cutter's soul.

Oliver paused on the porch of the shop, standing tall and gaunt among the clutter of sample stones. The porch was recessed under a wrought-iron balcony supported by ornate columns. He liked to stand on his porch and look out over the square. Almost directly across the square was the tall Oates Building. Farther down the street to his left there was the newspaper office. And, beyond that, the public library with its battlements, tower, and clock. Beyond the library, facing into the end of the square, there was Finkelstein's Pawn Shop, its windows filled with the shards of dreams. He turned to his right and looked at the city building, with its fire wagons and the patient powerful horses which pulled them.

In the center of the square, there was a strangely small and disproportionate court house, flanked by a spraying fountain and a monumental stone shaft. This latter, a memorial to a mountain hero, was a stubby obelisk, so ugly that it was beautiful.

And above and beyond and around the square were the mountains which ringed Asheville—hazy blue mountains that stood forever between him and the world.

He descended the steps and, with a long, easy stride, walked across the square, diagonally, past the fire station. This was

5

what Wolfe liked best: walking in the afternoon toward his house on Woodfin Street. He loved the house, with its fence, its marble steps going upward to the wide porch that crossed the front of the house and wrapped itself around one side. He loved his flowers, his fruit trees, the grapevine which had climbed a porch post, crossed the front of the house and let great clusters of grapes hang ripe and blue from the eaves.

He liked the fireplaces and the great fires he built in them. He liked its big kitchen, fragrant with cooking. He liked enormous quantities of food. Often he stopped at the markets to shop, or visited the farmers' wagons when they were parked on the square to sell fresh fruits and vegetables.

W. O. Wolfe loved many things in his world. But most of all he loved his children and his home. This was the core of his life, and he was its center.

Always, the children ran to greet him: his own and those of the neighbors. There was always much noise and laughter when he was with children. In the winter, after supper, they would gather round the fireplace and listen to Papa read from the Bible or quote long passages from Shakespeare or from "Horatio at the Bridge." In the summer, they would gather, usually along with adults from the neighborhood, on the broad front porch. They would stand leaning against the railing or sit on the steps to listen to stories of his travels. Papa was a traveller and a great teller of stories.

He often thought, on these walks home, of the wonder and strangeness of his life. And of the rude way in which fate and time had dealt with him. He was a man who had dreamed great dreams, but whose waking was a harsh disappointment.

As a boy he had wanted to be an actor. But his mother, knowing the fate of actors in nineteenth-century America, had been practical. She had apprenticed him to a stone-cutter. As a young man, he had learned his craft well: he was an excellent artisan. But his love for the stage, for the theatrical voice and gesture, never left him. His vision of the world became the dramatic vision. And his eyes sought the horizon.

His life was marred by marriage, too. His first wife had divorced him. His second wife's health had brought them to Asheville where they hoped the mountain air would be good for her. And after her long, lingering death, he was terribly alone.

With no children, W. O. Wolfe had been considered Asheville's most eligible widower. He had money, a good business, and, in his fine clothes, he was a handsome man. So he was not long single: pert, energetic Julia Westall became his third wife.

So now, in 1903, W. O. Wolfe walked toward his house and thought of the strangeness of time and of his happy brood of children. Each child was Papa's favorite; each had some special quality which allowed Oliver to say, "He's the best one of the bunch!" and mean every word of it.

There was Frank, whose life had been misshapen by his father's sporadic drinking. Frank all-too-frequently had to bring Oliver home when he'd had too much to drink. Poor Frank's life was a boasting waste, but his father saw even in him the virtue of persistent loyalty.

Then there was Effie. Effie was a quiet, competent girl who always did what was expected of her. She went softly through life, never reaching heights or depths. She was an obedient girl who sought only to please.

Her sister, Mabel, was perhaps Oliver's real favorite in most ways. She was volatile and earthy. She loved her family with a strange fierceness and loyalty. And even though it was Frank who brought Papa home from time to time, only Mabel could control him once he was in the house.

Next were the twins, Grover Cleveland and Benjamin Harrison. Grover was almost a sprite. Humorous, loving, laugh-

7

ing, chattering, Grover had a fine mind and a charming out-
look on the world. Papa had higher hopes for Grover than for
any of the others. He possessed all the qualities needed for
success in any undertaking.

His twin, Ben, was the strange one. He was the proud one,
with a dignity none of his brothers or sisters had. Unlike his
brothers and sisters, Ben had pale blue, quiet eyes and a sar-
donic, knowing smile. A firm reserve gave him a tough, resil-
ient exterior; inside was a hidden, profound caring which
time could never destroy.

And there was Fred, the noisy, stammering, born-salesman.
He always knew the treasures of the world were his for the
taking. And they would wait until he was ready to take them.
Fred had an explosive humor, with a touch of the clown, and
a warm love for the whole world.

And finally, Oliver thought as he turned onto Woodfin
Street, there was Tom. "What will Tom be like?" he asked
himself. Tom was only three, but he was Oliver's greatest
source of joy. When he was born, on October 3, 1900, they had
named him Thomas Clayton. But from birth he was Tom or
Tommy to the entire family.

Tom had bright, shiny eyes. They were brown, but there
was a light in them unlike the soft brownness of Grover's. He
had dark hair, which his mother carefully arranged in long,
shoulder-length curls. His lower lip was full and outthrust; it
was not a pouty lip, but a stubborn one.

Tom adored his Papa. He liked to be picked up by those
huge, strong stone-cutter's hands and tossed into the air. He
liked the abrasive afternoon beard when Papa nuzzled him.
He liked the attention, the care, his father gave him. And, at
the happy mealtimes, he liked the way his father would poke
around his stomach, then shout:

"Ah, there's an empty place! Have some more bread and
another spoon of mashed potatoes!" and he would begin to

heap more food on the child's plate. "Have some more milk, Tommy, and some of these good green beans."

And laughing happily, Tom would eat until he could hardly move.

Yet, Oliver's steps slowed as he approached his home. He was preoccupied and disturbed by Julia's plans for the summer. She was beginning to talk definitely now, as though her mind were clear at last.

For months, Julia had been thinking of going to St. Louis to the World's Fair. From coast to coast, America was singing "Meet Me in St. Louis." The country's eyes were on the great exposition and all the wonders it boasted of. It was Julia's idea to go to St. Louis, rent a large house, and provide room and board to the fair's visitors.

"Why, there'll be enough people there from Asheville to pay all our expenses," she'd said over and over. "I'll vow, Mr. Wolfe, I could pay every penny of the cost of the trip."

There was little doubt in his mind that she could. She was efficient and hard-working. She knew how to manage a house. She was an excellent cook. And she was a genius at making money.

They had argued about it for weeks. He was opposed to the idea, but not for reasons which gave substance to his arguments against it. So, as usual, he depended upon long harangues in which he predicted not only failure, but disaster. Yet, he knew that she would go and take the children with her.

The house on Woodfin Street would be a lonely place without his happy, noisy brood.

"Merciful God!" he stopped in front of the house, talking to himself. "Has it come to this? Am I to be abandoned to loneliness by an ungrateful family? It's too cruel! Oh, heartless woman! To leave a man helpless and alone in this place of desolation! Little did I know—"

9

He was surrounded now by happy, shouting children. And in their midst, he made his way up the marble steps and into the house, waving his arms theatrically and shouting against the cruelty of the world.

2

O, lost, and by the wind grieved, ghost come back again.

Look Homeward, Angel

THE LARGE BRICK HOUSE on Fairmount Avenue in St. Louis echoed with the shouts of five of the Wolfe children. Effie and Frank had stayed in Asheville with Papa. But Mabel, Ben and Grover, Fred and Tom were happy enough to make as much noise as the whole family ordinarily did.

They missed Effie and Frank, and they certainly missed Papa. But it was a blue sky world for most of the Wolfe family that summer of 1904. It was exciting enough just to live in this huge house and to meet new people every day.

But also, they visited the fair itself at least once a week and sometimes oftener. Fred and Grover were on the fairgrounds every day. In the fairgrounds hotel, called the Inside Inn, they had gotten jobs selling newspapers and magazines. Though Fred was only ten years old, he was possessed by a strong drive to sell. And, like Grover, he was friendly and vigorous. So he managed also to sell newspapers on a corner in downtown St. Louis.

Each day the boys would catch a trolley to go to their jobs. They were so friendly and so obviously industrious that they won the friendship and admiration of the trolley conductors. In almost no time, the conductors were refusing to accept fare from the two hard-working Wolfe boys.

In addition to the work, there was ample opportunity to have fun. Tom, almost four, played happily in the big house or on the large shady lawn. And there were exciting trips for him at least once each week.

With Ben holding his small hand, Tom would shriek as the ferris wheel on the midway of the fair plunged him downward. Once, in a dark tunnel, he was terrified beyond screaming as ghostly faces and frightening noises haunted him and the other passengers on the small boat which floated along the blackened passage.

And, on every visit to the fair, he would stand in awe before his favorite exhibit: a huge dragon-like locomotive, its pistons pumping and fire glowing from its belly as though it had eaten a piece of the earth's core.

Another favorite spot was the East India House, a part of the exhibit from India. Tom stared, open-mouthed, at the tall, turbaned waiters who served the rich aromatic tea which he loved.

And so the St. Louis summer passed. August lengthened its shadow toward September and the beginning of school. Oliver had visited them once during the summer, and Julia had promised to return to Asheville before the opening of school. Yet, as the time approached, she was unwilling to leave.

It was true, she knew, that there would be fewer visitors to the fair in the fall. Yet, if she were any judge, there would be a large enough number to justify her keeping the house a while longer. She had paid all their living expenses already, and had made a slight profit. A few more weeks would increase that profit substantially.

There was, she admitted to herself, the necessity of getting the children back in school.

"Mercy, it won't hurt 'em a bit to miss a few days of school," she told herself. "As the feller says, 'There's a lot more to education than what you can get from books.' I taught school myself, once, and, I tell you what, there's a lot to be said for experience. The fair's pretty educational, when you get right down to it."

She never made a definite decision; she simply let September come without actually deciding to go or to stay. And life on Fairmount Avenue continued without change until October.

When the change came in their lives, the Wolfes hardly noticed it. It was such a little thing: Grover began to lose interest in the job at the Inside Inn. Then his appetite began to diminish, and he lost his brightness.

One afternoon, he came home from the Inn early, complaining of a headache. He undressed and got into bed. Throughout the night, his sleep was fitful.

"Pshaw," Julia had said when he refused to come to supper. "There's nothing wrong with you that a little sleep won't cure. You're tired, that's all. You'll be up and rarin' to go in the morning. I tell you, there's nothing like a good night's sleep for a growing boy."

And she was right. The following morning, he was much better. During breakfast, he talked excitedly about going downtown. In a department store, he had seen a suit which he wanted very badly. Most of his earnings had gone into savings, but he had set aside a small amount each week to be applied to the purchase of the suit.

He and Mabel rushed through breakfast, then raced to the trolley stop. They chattered happily all the way downtown. In the department store, talking with the sales clerk about the suit, he was his old self again, happy and bright.

On the street again, the suit box under his arm, he walked jauntily along with Mabel. They passed a new sort of restaurant, unlike any they had ever seen before. It had a wide expanse of windows through which they could see the long counter with its round stools. Behind the counter, men dressed in white were making sandwiches.

There was a rule in the Wolfe family that the children were not to buy food in strange places. But this bright October day was a special day.

14

"Let's get something to eat," Grover said, then added in a grown up way, "I'll treat you to lunch."

So Grover and Mabel went into the lunchroom and climbed up on the stools. They looked at the menu painted on a big sign on the wall. Then, when the counterman walked over to them, they gave him their order.

They had just begun to eat when, without a word, Grover jumped off the stool and raced to the door. Mabel followed him as soon as she had picked up his suit box. He was standing at the curb, violently ill.

She helped him to the trolley stop. All the way to Fairmount Avenue, Grover's nausea became more violent. By the time they reached the house, he was trembling convulsively with chills.

Julia undressed him, got him into bed, and sent Mabel for Dr. Grudwell who lived only a few blocks away.

"You're going to be all right, Grover," Julia told him. "Why, you just ate something which disagreed with you. That's all. Why, just look how much better you felt this morning after a good night's sleep."

By the time the doctor had arrived, she was sure there was nothing wrong with Grover, except something he'd eaten.

Dr. Grudwell's examination was patient and thorough. He took Grover's temperature, scowling nearsightedly at the thermometer. He checked his pulse, listened to his heart, examined his mouth and throat.

"You're going to be all right, son," he patted Grover's shoulder. "You just try to get some sleep."

Julia followed him into the hall.

"That's exactly what I told him, Doctor," she said, closing the door to Grover's room. "A little sleep and rest is what he needs."

But when the doctor was alone with Julia, he said, "Grover's a mighty sick boy, Mrs. Wolfe."

"Why, Doctor, he's just got an upset stomach," Julia argued. "He just ate something that disagreed with him. I was saying just the other day—"

"Grover has typhoid," Dr. Grudwell interrupted her. "And it's as serious a case as I've ever seen."

Stunned, Julia listened to the doctor's instructions. As soon as he had left the house, promising to return that night, she set about the task of caring for him. She sent a telegram to Oliver, who came with Effie and Frank.

To her nursing of the sick boy, Julia brought an unqualified optimism. She was convinced that the illness was not as serious as the doctor had believed.

"I've seen lots of people get over sickness much worse than this," she said. "As the feller says, 'You've got to believe you're going to get well.' Believing is half the battle."

The house was hushed. The children went about subdued and quiet. Even Tom, who could not understand what had happened, was quiet as he played alone. The older children found no joy in the games which ordinarily delighted them. Ben, especially, retreated into silence.

After a few days, Grover's condition seem to improve. Julia's spirits rose in spite of Dr. Grudwell's pessimism: Grover would be all right.

Then one night in mid-November, his condition grew suddenly worse. His temperature rose sharply and his breath came in short, shallow gasps. Julia sent Ben, Frank, and Fred for the doctor.

Dr. Grudwell arrived in a matter of moments. He worked frantically with Grover, but all his efforts were in vain. Grover died a few moments past midnight.

"He was the best of the lot," wept Oliver. "That was the best boy a man could have."

The dreams he had dreamed for Grover went the way of

most of Oliver Wolfe's dreams. All the bright and happy promise was gone, almost before it had begun.

Julia was inconsolable.

"It's all my fault," she cried over and over. If only she hadn't come to St. Louis. If only she had returned to Asheville in August. If only she had been more careful. All the self-recrimination left her hollow-eyed and wan. She turned to her husband for comfort; but he could not find the words. He, who so loved the gesture of the dramatic, found that he had forgotten how to touch her shoulder or hold her hand. These two people, who needed each other's strength to carry them through this heavy November sadness, could not reach out anymore.

Always more terribly alone than they, Ben now withdrew further into the cold and friendless silence of himself. For the remainder of his life, Ben was locked within the prison of his loneliness. He could emerge only briefly for a clumsy gesture of affection for Fred or Tom.

Tom was too young to be aware of the significance of Grover's death. He knew only that he had not seen Grover for days. But he sensed somehow that he had suffered a wound from which he would never fully recover.

Grover's face would come to him in dreams. And he would remember his soft brown eyes and the happy whisper of his voice. And a quarter of a century later, he would cry, "Ghost, come back again!"

3

Beyond all misuse, pain, tragedy, death, confusion, necessity was on the rails. Not a sparrow fell through the air but that its repercussion acted on his life.

Look Homeward, Angel

TOM WAS REASSURED by the familiar rooms and furniture of
the house on Woodfin Street. During the St. Louis summer,
home had come to be only a memory as uncertain as the memory of a dream. His child mind had groped backward into
itself, trying to remember the wide porch, the marble block
which was the doorstop, the heavy oak table in the parlor. But
with the passing of each day, each object possessed less reality.

Now, back at home, Tom's first interest was in seeing and
touching all that he thought he had lost forever. He studied
the pattern of the carpet with its vivid colors. He touched the
cold marble of the table top. In the November cold, he looked
at the plum trees in the back yard and the high board fence
that closed the yard at the rear.

Each member of the family had absorbed the gall of his
own grief. And each in his loneliness sought, however clumsi-
ly, the love of the others. The Wolfe family moved into the
time of its warmest relationships. Never before, and never
again, would they be so close to one another.

Lost and lonely without his twin, Ben strengthened his love
for Tom. Tom was only four, and Ben was twelve. But the
difference in age served largely to increase Ben's competence
and concern. He poured out upon his small brother all the
love which would have gone to Grover. He had always been
able to handle Tom better than the others could. He played

with him, teased him, protected him. Tom grew to love very much this strange, quiet, and lonely brother who was so steady and dependable.

Fred, too, came into the warm relationship. Where Tom was concerned, Fred was capable of steadiness. But, unlike Ben, Fred was basically a comic character: he liked to laugh and to make others laugh. He was a born salesman, and, with his enormous vitality and his love of fun, he very early in life became what was in those days spoken of as a "real go-getter."

The year lengthened into winter and toward spring. The bowl of Asheville filled with snow. Then as the cycle swung round to spring, the thaws sent cascades of cold water splashing down the mountain. Summer came with heavy heat and straight downshaft of bright sun and throaty smell of hot weeds.

And the older children began to talk of school, with Tom listening enviously. All winter he had shared with them the great roaring fires Papa built and listened with them to his reading. In spring, they had shared bright blossoms and, in summer, shared the drowsy afternoons. And now he wanted more than anything to join them at school.

Julia reluctantly permitted it. It represented his first long step away from her. Like most mothers, she dreaded the loss of her baby. That he would grow away from her was inevitable, of course, but she wanted to postpone it as long as possible. By the time Ben added his pleas to Tom's, and Papa added his insistence, the battle was won.

Each morning Tom would rush through his breakfast with his older brothers and sisters. Ben would dress him, comb his hair, and shine his shoes. Then they would troop off together to Orange Street School.

At first, the big building frightened and confused him. It had great high windows, long corridors, many doors. But he loved the excitement, the smell of chalk, the complexities of learning. Ben helped him learn his way around the building, and served as a quiet protector against the inevitable school bullies.

For weeks, Tom and the other first graders listened in awe to the tales of the other children. Usually, these stories centered on Mr. Roberts, the principal. According to the older children, The Principal was larger than life, an avenging angel who knew one's most secret thoughts, and whose punishments were as severe as his judgment was inflexible. Discipline in the classroom was usually begun with a threat to send the offender to The Principal's Office, which was looked upon as a sort of purgatory.

Actually, J. M. Roberts was a rare breed of man who never quite achieved success in the world's terms. If he had dreamed the dreams of youth, they surely did not end with Orange Street School. Yet, this is where he found himself, and there seemed to be no door to a wider or richer world.

This sensitive and dedicated man poured himself out to the children who could not receive what he had to give. His mind and spirit soared above and beyond the mountain rims, where the children could not follow. Roberts was delighted when he could reach out and communicate with the rare child that could appreciate what he had to give. But for the most part, he carried his duties as the principal as a heavy cross that he bore to the calvary of his failure.

But Tom was unaware of this. He merely saw Mr. Roberts as a man of authority. And Tom saw school as a place to learn a language. For Tom Wolfe was already searching for a way to reach beyond the lonely prison of self.

With school as an added dimension, Tom's life began to round out to full. There was play and work after school. There were his boisterous brothers and sisters around the table at mealtime. In the evenings, there was homework. And, always, Papa's stories around the fire. Frequently, Mabel played the piano, or, more often, sang while Effie played.

Julia thought more and more frequently of her St. Louis experiment. As the shock of Grover's death diminished to a dull ache, she began to search for ways to keep herself busy. And she was always interested in making money. She had proved, in St. Louis at least, that she could operate a boarding house profitably. If she could do it in St. Louis, she said to herself, she could do it in Asheville.

This little town cupped in the mountains was experiencing a growing popularity as a vacation spot. Also, Asheville was becoming well known as a resort for persons ill with respiratory diseases. The number of boarding houses was increasing daily, and Julia wanted to get her's started before competition became too severe.

For weeks, she had considered all the arguments for and against the starting of the business. Then she began to look at houses which would meet her requirements. And finally, in 1906, she bought a huge house on Spruce Street. Over its steps she hung a sign: "The Old Kentucky Home."

"Merciful God!" roared Oliver when he learned of it. "You'll destroy us! O, that I should live to see the day! Little did I know, woman, that you would ever bring me so low as this."

"There's nothing low about providing room and board to decent, respectable people," Julia answered.

"To sell one's hospitality," bellowed her husband. "For a pittance, to sell one's home and food. O, vilest of the vile! To have my family destroyed by those incarnate fiends of hell who will live in that murderous and bloody barn."

Night after night, the shouting and roaring went on. He would stride back and forth across the room, flinging his arms out, shaking his fist, pointing a long finger at Julia, and bellowing accusations.

23

Julia answered his charges in a quiet voice. And the softness of her answers, the obstinacy of her mind, infuriated him all the more. Both Julia and Oliver knew that, in the end, neither would change his point of view. Their lives were following divergent paths and neither could alter his course.

Julia's purchase of the Spruce Street property came as near as anything ever would to shattering the Wolfe family. Oliver refused to move from his beloved home on Woodfin Street to live in the "murderous and bloody barn." Mabel would not abandon him to live alone on Woodfin Street, so she, too, refused to move. Tom was still too small to be away from his mother and so was taken to live in what he later described as a "great, chill tomb." The other children were not even considered: they wandered from one house to another, depending upon the mood of the moment.

The closeness of the family had been the center of Tom's life, the nucleus around which his spirit was developing. This unnecessary fragmentation of the family left him unprotected and alone. He had, he later said, "two roofs and no home." He preferred the house on Woodfin Street. And, though he actually lived in the boarding house, he spent many hours in his father's house, and Mabel always saw to it that its doors were never locked.

Tom hated The Old Kentucky Home. It was shabby and cold. He disliked the people who rented rooms there. They were old or ill, they rocked in the chairs on the porch, and spent their days complaining.

Julia's thriftiness became niggardliness. Since her profit depended almost entirely on low overhead, she saved in every way possible. Accustomed to his father's generosity, Tom began to despise his mother's frugality. And he felt, as his father did, that operating a boarding house carried with it a stigma which was visible to all and a source of humiliation.

Tom spent as little time as possible at the boarding house.

As soon as school was out each afternoon, he would race to Woodfin Street. In the big, friendly kitchen, Mabel would prepare an after-school snack for him, and, while he ate, she would ask him about school.

He liked also to go to his father's shop on the square. He loved the two-storied building with its cluttered porch. He liked the dusty, musty smell of the place, the spongy wooden floors, the cluttered office. Most of all, though, he liked the workshop at the rear of the building.

It was here that his father drew designs on slabs of stone and carved them. There were chisels and mallets and emery wheels scattered about the place. Oliver Wolfe used no machinery: all the work in his shop was done with chisels driven by great wooden mallets. He preferred wood to steel because he could get a softer touch with them.

Tom loved to watch his father work. Wearing a long apron, Mr. Wolfe would bend his six-foot-four frame over a block of marble. With firm strokes of the mallet, he would cause to appear beneath the chisel doves, wreaths of flowers, clasped hands, and other tombstone designs.

Several times each week, after an hour in the shop, Tom would visit the public library. Tom could not remember a time when his father did not read to his children from the Bible, from Shakespeare, or Thomas Grey, or Macauley. Now that he could read for himself, the public library became a place of wonder.

The long shelves, the high ceilings, the massive oak tables and chairs, the buckram and leather smell of the place all excited him. The massed rows of books were almost a challenge to his appetite. He began to try to read every book in the library, hoping that he would find in some of them "the great forgotten language and the lost lane-end into heaven."

This appetite for books was never completely satisfied. Later, as a student at the university and in the great cities he visited as an adult, he saw libraries as something to be consumed.

For some time, Fred had been the Asheville representative of the Curtis Publishing Company. With his love for people, his outgoing manner, and his drive to excel, Fred was a fine salesman. It was just a matter of time until he had employed a dozen or so boys to do the selling for him, while he assumed the role of head of the local Curtis agency.

Each week, he received from the company a summary of the current issue of the *Saturday Evening Post* and a preview of the next. He would read each of these carefully, rephrase them in his own words, and insist that the boys commit the new version to memory. The result was that when Fred's little band of salesmen went onto the streets, they had an impressive sales talk.

None of them, however, was as effective as Fred himself. He would attach himself to a passerby and begin telling him about the most recent issue. About the only way the victim could rid himself of Fred Wolfe was to give up and buy a magazine from him. He trained his boys to employ the same technique. The result was that in Asheville almost everyone read Curtis publications.

It wasn't long until Tom was recruited into Fred's sales force. He loathed selling, but he felt compelled to perform as Fred wanted him to. Perhaps it was a simple matter of justifying himself in his brother's estimation. Or perhaps Fred was extraordinarily successful in instilling in all his boys a fierce competitive spirit.

Whatever the cause, Tom became a good magazine salesman. In a letter to his sister, Effie, he wrote, "I sold 61 Posts this week. Fred is going to give the boys who sell the most Posts this week 50 cents, but I ain't in it. If I was I would beat them all to pieces. So he don't want me in it. The boys would not feel like working if I beet them."

Though his grammar and spelling were not the best, his magazine sales apparently were.

The years walked by the Wolfes with soft but certain steps. Tom's awareness of the flow of time was increasing: he saw it as an endless river flowing without ceasing or slowing. In the course of the flow, the Wolfes had sustained two severe injuries: Grover's death and the shattering of solidarity which was the inevitable result of the opening of the Old Kentucky Home. Yet each of them managed to adapt to the unusual conditions which life had imposed upon them.

Ben had begun to work for the Asheville newspaper and was growing toward a dignified manhood. Effie had married and moved to South Carolina. Mabel, with Pearl Shope as her partner, was touring the South, singing in hotels and night clubs. Fred's magazine business prospered as his salesmanship was refined by his constant efforts at self improvement.

Oliver was living out his lonely life on Woodfin Street, unaware that within him strange, malignant cells were forming, which would spread until his great body was destroyed. He emerged from his loneliness only for an occasional visit to the Old Kentucky Home or for an epic drinking spree.

Julia began to be plagued by rheumatism, and, during the winter months when there were too few tourists to keep her occupied, she began to travel. Always, of course, she took Tom with her. At various times, they went to New Orleans, St. Petersburg, Palm Beach, and Washington. Tom's school work did not suffer from these midwinter vacations.

At times, though, Julia's frugality subjected Tom to some humiliating experiences. On one of their trips to Florida, for instance, Julia's thriftiness was offended by the sight of coconuts wasting on lawns where they had fallen from the trees. She secured some gunny sacks and set Tom to the task of gathering them.

"Lands sakes, boy," she told him, "those people don't want

them, or they wouldn't have left them laying out there to spoil. They won't mind you taking them. You'll be doing them a favor, as the feller says."

But even with such humiliating moments, when his face reddened with shame, and his throat constricted as he tried to keep from crying, the trips were a source of great joy for Tom. They took him into the wide and wonderful world beyond the jagged prison walls of his mountains. All his life, he had heard the sagas of his father's travels to distant cities. Now he himself was the far-wanderer, searching for himself and for the meaning of his life in the dark strangeness of the South.

As long as he lived, Thomas Wolfe's heart beat to the rhythm of the pounding wheels of America's great trains. The lonely cry of a locomotive in the night would always call up a host of memories, or summon dreams of cities unknown to him. As a man, he would at times compile lists of America's cities, rivers and mountains, names which evoked visions of all the places he had yet to see. As long as he lived, Tom was part wanderer, searching forever for "a stone, a leaf, a door."

Travel no doubt improved Tom's powers of observation and his ability to draw conclusions from what he observed. At school, Mr. Roberts, always alert for exceptional brightness in his pupils, had on several occasions been impressed by the ability of this strange little boy.

Once, Tom wrote about what he saw in a painting. So perceptive and so sensitive was his paper that Roberts took it home in order that his wife Margaret, also a teacher, might read it. She saw immediately that Thomas Wolfe possessed an extraordinary talent.

In 1912, just before Tom's twelfth birthday, J. M. Roberts announced his resignation as public school principal. He had completed his plans to open a private school. He had bought a large house, repainted it, and announced the plans for The North State Fitting School.

It was to be expected that the Roberts would want Tom in their student body. There was much discussion about it: some of the Wolfe family felt that they should not put on airs by enrolling Tom in a private school. There was some jealousy, too: all the others had gone to public school. Why should Tom have this unnecessary privilege?

J. M. Roberts talked to Oliver about it, telling him of his belief that Tom was too good a student to remain in public school. Oliver, remembering the shattering of his dreams for Grover, saw that perhaps Tom would be the one to bring credit to the family. His decision was that Tom would enter the first class to be enrolled at The North State Fitting School.

Besides his immediate family, three people in Tom's life would mold and shape him: his editor, the woman he loved, and his first important teacher—Margaret Roberts. She became the center his life lacked, and she saw him as no one else had. Her angle of vision was from Tom's center: she saw him whole and clear, and helped him to see himself.

She taught him history, English literature, and composition. But the facts and skills imparted in the classroom were the least significant things she gave him. For, like all good teachers, she exerted upon him an unseen influence, bringing him around to the best in himself.

She gently pointed out how his writing could be improved. Without seeming to lead him, she led him. She brought him to good books: to this point in his life, Tom had read voraciously but indiscriminately. She helped him to discover the great writers and to relate their fine books with others. Through her, Tom learned to reject the cheap and the shabby, to search for and love all that was beautiful, and to set high standards for his own performance.

She helped him, too, in the difficult task of changing from child to adolescent. Julia, with much regret and lamentation, had acknowledged his age. All his life, she had wanted him to

29

remain in perpetual babyhood. His long curls were a constant symbol of his status: Mama's Baby Boy. Now she had permitted them to be cut. With his long curls gone, he had partially broken the fetters that bound him. But he was never to get away from his babyhood entirely.

By the time he was fourteen, Tom was unusually tall. His bones and frame were large, but they supported very little flesh or muscle. His legs were long, somewhat out of proportion to his trunk, and he bounded along the shady streets with great loping strides. His head was too large for his body, but his face, delicately sculptured, was too small for his head. In his own words, "it seemed not to belong to his body." His eyes lost their mellowness: as his intensity of spirit increased, a fierce fire glowed in his brown eyes.

It was inevitable that Julia would associate Tom's growth with responsibility and responsibility with earning power. It did not occur to her that Tom needed rest and sleep more than he needed to earn money.

"Lands sakes, boy," she kept telling him, "it's time you started bringing in some money. As the feller says, you're getting big enough to pay for your keep."

Tom started delivering the Asheville Citizen, which was more lucrative than selling magazines for Fred. So every morning, he rose before dawn to deliver his papers. He enjoyed being up and at work when others were sleeping. He would walk down the streets, past sleep-shut houses, into the Square. Beyond the splashing fountain, his father's shop stood dark and silent. A small cafe was open, and a few early risers would be huddled over its counter.

He would go to the paper office. The big press was silent. The mailing clerks would be putting rolled newspapers into the big gray mail sacks; his scowling brother, Ben, would be nagging the carrier boys, snarling at them, urging them to hurry. The floor was littered with newsprint; the building was permeated with the rich fragrance of ink and paper.

He would sling his paperbag over his shoulder and lunge back out into the morning. His route carried him down the wet, winding streets and alleys of Asheville's Negro section. Here, there were unpainted wooden shacks with snaggle-toothed fences, grassless yards, sagging porches toward which he hurled his folded papers.

Tom generally enjoyed these dawn-dark hours, the sound of his feet in the morning silence, the sun coming up over the fog-heavy mountain peaks. And if, inside the shut houses, men and women dreamed, none of them dreamed in sleep as richly as did this boy who tossed the papers onto their porches. For his dreams were of fame and fortune beyond all description.

In spite of the drain on his energy, Tom flourished academically. As the spring of 1916 approached, his reputation as a good student was firmly established. He was only fifteen years old, but he was ready for graduation. Though he had not yet discussed it with his parents, he wanted to attend the University of Virginia.

During the last semester of his senior year, Tom entered a contest sponsored by the *Independent Magazine*. His entry was on "Shakespeare, The Man."

Tom concentrated on the spirit of Shakespeare. Other entries were more accurate and more detailed in presenting the essential facts of Shakespeare's life. Some were more scrupulous in the presentation of detail. But, in the opinion of the panel of judges, none was so sympathetic nor so understanding of the essential quality of the man; Tom's essay won first prize. The bronze medal was the first public recognition his writing ever received.

Shortly after the close of the contest, the school sponsored a "declamation" contest. Tom overcame the stammer which

31

characterized his normal speech and read his Shakespeare essay for this contest. He won another first prize.

The entire Wolfe family basked in Tom's glory. Oliver, especially, was delighted. His love for Shakespeare and for oratory led him to consider Tom's twin prizes as truly extraordinary. He began to see in Tom possibilities for achievement in everything in which he himself had failed. He quickly convinced himself that Tom's best future lay in politics, and the road to politics was the law. Thomas Wolfe, his father decided, would be a lawyer and a politician and, ultimately, governor of the state.

Tom accepted this readily enough. At fifteen, he had given little thought to what he wanted to do. He knew only that there was a world to be seen and conquered. It lay beyond the wall of the mountain, waiting for him. His dreams were of fame and fortune, of gold and glory. It seemed reasonable that these could be obtained through the law and politics.

At graduation time that spring, Tom's emotions were sharply divided. He was eager to conquer his share of the world. But his heart was heavy at the thought of leaving his family, his familiar town, his mountains.

But he knew that one day he would return, rich and famous.

4

He was a child when he went away: he was a child who had looked much on pain and evil and remained a fantasist of the ideal. . . . He belonged, perhaps to an older and simpler race of men: he belonged with the Mythmakers.

Look Homeward, Angel

DECISIONS WERE NEVER EASILY MADE in the Wolfe family. Most families discuss problems quietly, reach decisions rationally. Among the Wolfes, problem-solving took the form of hysteria. Reason was abandoned, and the din could be heard clearly by neighbors on both sides of the house.

Consideration of college for Tom constituted a crisis. Tom chose the University of Virginia, largely because it was considerable distance from Asheville and partly because he had friends who were enrolled there.

His father insisted that he attend the University of North Carolina. Oliver's reasons were more practical than Tom's. If a man is going to be a politician, he must have a firm home base, which he can best build in his own state university.

His arguments failed to convince Tom. Tom was burdened not only by this disagreement with his father, but also by his guilt feelings about going to college at all. None of the other children had been given a similar opportunity by Mr. Wolfe or Julia, and Tom sensed their resentment.

Only Ben offered him any real encouragement.

"For God's sake, go to college," Ben urged. "None of the rest of us ever got a thing from them. Take everything they'll give you. Go to college. It's the only chance you've got to get away."

When Oliver's arguments failed to convince Tom that he

should go to the University of North Carolina, Mr. Wolfe called up reinforcements. Among these was Mabel, who was now married to Ralph Wheaton and living in Raleigh. Since Raleigh is not far from Chapel Hill, site of the university, Oliver thought the prospect of being near his sister would appeal to Tom.

When Mabel and Ralph came to Asheville, specifically for the purpose of helping convince Tom, Mabel's approach was not nearly as subtle as merely suggesting that Tom would enjoy visiting her on weekends.

"Now, you look here," she pointed her finger at Tom. "Just because you did pretty well at the Roberts' school is no reason for you to be so high and mighty now. You ought to think about what Papa says."

"Mabel, I'm not being high and mighty," Tom tried to explain. "All the boys at Charlottesville—"

"You just forget your high-toned friends," Mabel interrupted. "Just remember that none of the rest of us had this kind of chance. Just remember that, Mister High-and-Mighty. This family has been darn good to you and don't you forget it."

Their argument became heated, but Tom's position remained unchanged. Now Oliver began to bring in friends and neighbors whose opinions he thought Tom would respect. They were in solid agreement. The young man looking toward a career in law and politics should make lasting contacts within the state. The people he would meet, the friends he would make at the University of North Carolina, would ultimately become the opinion-makers of the state. Tom, they agreed, should not go to the University of Virginia.

Still Tom was adamant, and, as September drew near, Oliver brought up his last line of argument:

"Your choice is easy, Son," he said. "Either you go to the University of North Carolina, or you don't go at all."

Within two weeks, Tom was enrolled at the University of North Carolina.

"I arrived at my decision to attend our state university last Wednesday night," he wrote to Ralph Wheaton. "Perhaps I should say forced instead of arrived, for that is what it amounted to. For I had held out for the University of Virginia in spite of the family's protests. But when no reply came from the University of Virginia, I consented to go to Carolina."

The University of North Carolina, founded in 1792, is the oldest of the state universities. Its campus is broad and beautiful and campus life is rich in tradition. The beautiful arching trees surround buildings with stark lines and simple grace. Chapel Hill was a village with little meaning except in terms of the university. Like most Carolinians, Tom came to love the place dearly.

But in the fall of 1916 when, in his own words, he was "the greenest of the green freshmen," he hated it. He was barely sixteen and he brought mountaineer strangeness with him from Asheville. He was the natural victim of several sophomore harassments.

He had not been on the campus a week when he was warned by a sophomore about the importance of the "catalogue examination." Heeding the prankster's advice, Tom spent hours memorizing the contents of the university catalogues in order to pass an examination which, of course, was never given. On another occasion, he was led off to chapel to hear a sermon delivered by a distinguished and bearded faculty member . . . who turned out to be a student in disguise.

When along with fifty others, he was inducted into the Dialectic Literary Society, he was the only one of the new members who was ill-informed enough to think an acceptance speech was in order. The members of the organization and the other inductees listened with good breeding as the tall, stam-

mering oaf from the mountains delivered a grandiose acceptance address.

Tom survived the practical jokes and his own naiveté and
the first term of school. He thrived on the Dialectic Literary
Society and the Freshman Debating Club. He had always enjoyed talking, and, even though he had a pronounced stammer, these two organizations provided most of the happiness
he experienced during his freshman year.

Julia visited the campus to see her "baby" and, as usual,
she humiliated him. She met most of his friends and some of
his instructors, and she insisted on soliciting business from
them.

"I declare," she would say to them. "If you can drum up
some business for me at the boarding house, why, as the feller
says, I'll give you free room and board if you're ever in Asheville."

Tom twisted up inside himself at this crass attitude toward
his friends and at the shabbiness of her trying to use them to
get business for a boarding house. Like his father, he despised
the idea of selling hospitality. And he resented, far more
strongly than he could say, that his friends would be welcome
in his home only as paying guests or as agents for the business
to be paid off in room and board.

It might have been this sort of thing that contributed most
to his decision not to return to the University of North Carolina for his sophomore year. Instead of the University of Virginia, this time he would try for a school farther away:
Princeton. During the second semester of this first year at Carolina, he began to lay careful plans by which he hoped to
convince his father that he should go to Princeton the second
year. He won Mabel over to his side, along with some of his
teachers. He was not at all sure of victory, but he hoped at
least to lay a solid foundation for a change of school in his
junior year.

Before school closed, the United States had entered the war against Germany. The country was in a state of euphoria, part confusion, part fear, part patriotism. The people were absorbed in the tasks of war, and all the young men were eager to join the army.

Tom was too young for military service, so he spent the summer at home in Asheville. Fred had enlisted in the Navy. Ben, whose dignity and sense of worth rested on a fierce scornful pride, needed to be accepted for military service to shore up his self respect.

But Ben was probably already a victim of tuberculosis. He was thin, sallow, hollow-chested, a constant smoker of cigarettes. The examining physician reported that Ben's lungs were in far from satisfactory condition, and he was rejected for service in the army. It is difficult in wartime to explain one's civilian status. In people's eyes, there is always the unspoken question, and scornful defiance is always the unspoken answer.

Ben was moody, morose, more cynical than usual. His love for Tom was unchanged, but he was clumsier and gruffer in his attempts to express it.

Oliver was ill . . . too ill to live alone in the big old house on Woodfin Street. Julia was too busy with the season's boarders to care for him. Poor Mabel was again called on to sacrifice her own wishes for the good of her father. She left her husband in Raleigh and came to Asheville to care for Oliver. She saw Ralph only as often as he could drive to Asheville.

Tom was the one to whom Mabel turned.

"When will I ever have a life of my own?" she would cry. "How much longer will I have to take care of everybody but myself? Oh, I don't mind taking care of Papa. But why can't somebody else do their part? Why must I do it all?"

Regardless of where he turned, Tom breathed the stale air of frustration, tension, anger. Throughout the Old Kentucky

Home there was a climate of death and despair. On Woodfin Street, Oliver complained of the pain, Mabel of the unfairness of it all.

Among the guests at the boarding house, though, there was a bright, happy girl. Clara Paul, only a year or so out of her teens, had brought her younger brother to Asheville to recuperate from a serious illness. Tom turned to her for friendship and for moments of happiness in an otherwise wretched summer.

Clara was engaged to be married in the fall. She spoke from time to time of her fiance and of their plans. But such talk fell on deaf ears as far as Tom was concerned. He was much too lonely to think of her marriage. He thought of her only in terms of his own need.

Clara endeared herself to all who knew her through her spontaneity and her natural optimism. She found the boarders interesting people. She liked to talk with them, to listen to their problems. She enjoyed helping Mrs. Wolfe with the work of the place, and she was lovingly solicitous of her younger brother, whom Tom generally ignored.

Tom thought Clara was beautiful. She had close cut cornsilk hair, and a scattering of freckles across her nose, and a dawn smile.

That she liked Tom is beyond question. They went on picnics and took long walks and sat for hours on the porch of the Old Kentucky Home. They talked of Tom's year at college. He told her of his plans for the future, his hopes of going to Princeton, his dreams of success. She listened with concern and understanding.

Tom fell deeply in love for the first time. He was alternately happy and miserable, hopeful and despairing, talkative and taciturn. Clara had certainly not concealed her plans from him. He knew she was expecting to be married; he hoped his love for her would be strong enough to prevent it.

Meanwhile—and he talked to her about it—he was working up his courage to discuss with his father his desire to go to Princeton. And, late in the summer, he was forced to bring it up earlier than he had anticipated: Oliver's illness became worse. His cancer was spreading, and it was hoped that radium treatments would arrest its spead.

"Merciful God!" roared the sick man at Tom's first mere mention of Princeton. "I won't hear any more. Not another word. Go to Chapel Hill or stay in Asheville. That's the choice. Leave me alone."

And so, at the end of the summer, Tom prepared to return to Chapel Hill. He later wrote of the coming of September, "full of departing wings." It was a time of sad partings. Mabel and Ben took Mr. Wolfe to Baltimore for radium treatments. Clara Paul went to Norfolk to be married, and Tom returned to Chapel Hill.

The return to Chapel Hill was more pleasant than he had anticipated. For one thing, it was a relief just to be away from the tensions and conflicts of Asheville. For another, the sophomore year was more bearable than the freshman year had been.

The campus seemed less hostile. Indeed, it was familiar and almost friendly. Tom was secretly pleased that so many people remembered him and seemed glad to see him again. His loneliness was made less acute by his sharing a room with another boy from Asheville, Edmund Burdick. Burdick was a quiet, friendly fellow. He was steady and dependable, and he liked and admired Tom. While he was never among Tom's best friends, they were close, and Tom found him to be a person in whom he could confide.

Now that he was a sophomore, Tom was more sure of himself and, as the semester's activities got underway, he began to involve himself in school affairs. He began to write, for instance, for the *Tar Heel*, the university's weekly four-page newspaper. He also started contributing to the *Carolina Magazine*, the school's literary journal. As his work grew in intensity and difficulty, his enormous energy increased to meet the demands.

Tom always liked to talk, and he would seek out bull sessions at the YMCA or in student rooms at all hours of the night. Or he would go to an all-night cafe to eat or to drink coffee and talk with anyone who had the time and the interest.

His tall figure bounding with great strides across the campus became a familiar and somewhat startling sight. He had grown considerably taller, but had gained no weight. His height was becoming a source of frustration, and he was beginning to consider it a physical handicap. As his height went past six-feet-four, he discovered that beds were too short, door openings too low, automobiles too crowded, classroom desks too small. The world, he later said, was designed for men five-feet-six and he was six-feet-five.

People constantly stared at him, and the crude ones enjoyed smart questions. "Hey, Buddy, how's the weather up there?" was always good for a laugh. Harder to bear were the stares of the curious. He came to experience the anguish of the lame: the knowledge that his physical appearance set him apart as surely as though he were a freak on the planked stage of the carnival midway. Ten years later, he would say that he had something in common with a crippled student who limped badly: both had physical handicaps.

Without knowing it, Tom was partly responsible for the attention he drew. He had little money, and he never cared about clothes, except in the severely practical sense, so he was rarely well-dressed. His coats and trousers were always too small. Part of the cause of this was that he could not afford to have clothes custom made. There was always difficulty in finding clothes, designed for a thin person almost six and a half feet tall, on the department store racks. Part of the problem, also, was that many of his clothes were gifts.

While he was at home during the Christmas holiday, Ben had said something about one of his own suits which he no longer wore. A few weeks later, Tom wrote to Ben about the suit, asking if he might have it. "Most of my stuff is frayed," he told Ben. "If you don't need that particular suit, I would be more than thankful to get it."

Ben mailed the suit to him. Since there was considerable difference in their sizes, the suit did not fit at all well. But Tom happily wore it, rarely having it cleaned or pressed.

Tom was frequently shabby. His shirts were usually rumpled and soiled, his ties stringy, wrinkled, and spotty. He rarely remembered to have his hair cut so it was always down over his ears and collar.

To make his clothing problem even more difficult, he would not put things away. He usually dropped each item of clothing on the floor or over a chair wherever he happened to be standing when he took it off. Occasionally, he would kick an article of clothing under the bed.

On one occasion, a friend was waiting for Tom while he packed for a trip to Asheville. The friend was surprised, to say the least, at Tom's method of packing a bag. He opened the suitcase on the floor, gathering shirts and other items of clothing from under the bed. He flung these along with clean clothes from a dresser drawer into the suitcase. When the bag would not close, he stamped several times on the clothing to pack it down. Then he forced the bag closed and was ready to leave.

Tom was as careless about time as he was about clothing. In his later writing he was obsessed with "time like a great river flowing." He thought of time in terms of the sweep of planets, the appearance once-a-century of comets, the crumbling of mountain ranges, the wash of ocean tides. But he never grasped the significance of minutes and hours.

He frequently would forget to eat lunch and dinner, then during a midnight conversation, would suddenly remember. He was often late to his classes. He was habitually late, sometimes by hours, sometimes by a whole day, for many appointments he had made in good faith.

His tendency to ignore deadlines for submission of copy to the *Tar Heel* would leave its editor quivering with rage.

Early in the second semester of his sophomore year, Tom's popularity brought him membership in Pi Kappa Phi, a social fraternity. At about the same time, he was initiated into Sigma Epsilon, scholastic fraternity.

That spring, his first strictly literary effort was published in the *Carolina Magazine*. The first piece was a poem called "The Challenge." It was intensely patriotic, highly imitative, stilted, and trite. But Tom was sufficiently proud of it to send a copy of the issue to his father. The same issue of the magazine included his first published fiction: a short story called "A Cullenden of Virginia."

Tom was later to talk about these early efforts with a great sense of humor, especially making fun of the sentimental sort of patroitism expressed in the poem. But they were a beginning.

Tom's happy and productive year was drawing to a close. There had been little to mar his serenity. Then, his roommate, of whom he had grown protectively fond, suffered a heart attack. The shock of his death was almost more than Tom could bear. He refused to re-enter the room they had shared, and some of his friends put cots in their rooms for Tom. For the remainder of the year, Tom slept first in one room then in another.

He wanted school to come to a close. Yet, he dreaded going back to Asheville for the summer. The bitterness and pain of the previous summer was an experience he did not want to repeat. So he began to cast about for ways to avoid Asheville. He also sought for ways to earn money in order to be more independent of his family the following year.

When school was out, therefore, he went to Norfolk. He hoped to find a job and to see Fred, who was stationed at a naval base nearby.

Perhaps the strongest attraction for him in Norfolk was the hope of seeing again the young girl, Clara Paul, whom he had met the summer before at his mother's boarding house.

5

He came, a god with broken feet, into the gray hovel of this world. And he lived here a stranger, trying to recapture the music of the lost world, trying to recall the great forgotten language, the lost faces, the stone, the leaf, the door.

Look Homeward, Angel

NORFOLK, IN THE SUMMER OF 1918, was a roaring confusion. The war effort was at its best and worst there, and Tom found that getting a job was not as easy as it sounded. He had hoped to get a job as a carpenter. But he had neither training nor experience, and could not qualify.

The best he could do was to find a job as timekeeper for a gang of laborers. The job was alternately dull and infuriating. The workers were illiterate, lazy, and crude. The pay was so low that he could barely make ends meet, so he began to look for a better job.

After a few days, he found a job checking supplies at the naval base at Newport News. The first days were almost unbearable. After he had paid his room rent in advance, he had little left for food. Almost all his money from the first job was gone, and it was two weeks before he could collect his pay for the checker's job.

Eventually, hunger became stronger than pride. Tom and several of his equally hungry friends went to the base proper, searching for Fred. Fred was delighted to see his kid brother, and he immediately sensed what the problem was.

"I was right much of a politician at the base already," Fred later told Mabel. "I had several friends who were cooks back at the galley. That's where I took Tom and his friends."

"Mabel," he continued, "I'll never forget the meal those

boys ate. It seemed to me they were actually famished. I doubt that they had a square meal since getting to Norfolk. Anyway, I really enjoyed watching those boys eat. Later it did come out that all they had was a can of beans a day apiece and a loaf of bread split between them. They had been too proud to come to me for a little help while they waited for their pay."

Tom continued to check supplies at the Newport News base. After receiving his first paycheck, he had enough money to get by on and a bit to save toward the next year's college expenses.

In his off-duty hours, he occasionally saw Fred. But more often, he explored the sprawling installation at Newport News, walked the piers, or wandered through the streets. He was much aware of the nearness of Clara. He thought almost constantly of going to see her. He made up fantasies about how glad she would be to see him, and how sad she would be that she had married the wrong man.

His indecision about seeing her was painful. Part of him wanted desperately to see her. Another part was afraid of a rebuff or of the depression he knew he would experience once he had seen her and had left her again. So all summer he worked, and at night was dream-haunted as he stalked the docks in his loneliness.

He returned to Chapel Hill without having seen Clara. Within a few months, she was dead, a victim of an influenza epidemic.

Hardly had the fall semester of 1918 begun when Tom received a telegram from his mother urging him to come home at once. Ben was dying.

The trip to Asheville was a long one. Tom had time to think, and thinking took the form of memory. Tom's memory, like that of his mother, was one of total recall. The past flowed back upon him like the back wash of a tide, engulfing him in its strangeness. Going back to see Ben, he relived moment after moment, each revealing some facet of his relationship with his scowling, scornful brother.

When Tom was small, his mother was too busy to give him the care he needed. It was Ben who helped him; Tom rejected aid from any of the others. But Ben could handle him, and the two drew close in the strangeness and bitterness of their world.

Tom remembered Ben dressing him before he could do it for himself. Ben took a fierce pride in having his little brother neat, clean, well-dressed. With painful clarity, Tom remembered Ben kneeling in front of him, his eyes intent upon his fingers and the buttons they worked with. Ben had a way of fastening upon things with his eyes, holding the things close as though with his eyes he could prevent their moving.

He would dress Tom, and when the task was done, his eyes, gentle yet scornful, looked deep into Tom's.

"Now, you look all right," he would say. "Try to stay that way," and he would add with mock sternness, "you little fool."

Tom remembered the black, pointed-toed shoes Ben had bought for himself. Ben was proud of the shoes, which were in the height of fashion when he bought them. But they were too small, and, after a few days, he stopped wearing them. Into his closet they went, and he had almost forgotten about them.

"I declare, I wish I was rich enough to throw shoes away," Julia said to him one day. "I guess you rich folks can afford to buy fancy shoes and not wear them."

Thereupon, she had made Tom wear the shoes. She hadn't found it necessary to force Tom to take them. He was pleased to have such fashionable footwear, even if they did hurt his feet. His feet were as big as Ben's by this time, so the shoes did not fit him any better than they fit Ben.

But Tom continued to wear them. Day after day, Ben scowled and snarled as Tom hobbled around the house, wincing with every step. Finally he could bear it no longer.

"Take those shoes off, you fool," he snarled at Tom. Then he turned on Julia: "For God's sake, Mama, buy the boy a pair of shoes. You've got the money. Or do you want to make a cripple out of him just to save a few dollars?"

Tom got new shoes.

Only last spring, Tom had gone to Winston-Salem to visit Ben during the Easter holidays. It had been a wonderful weekend for the two brothers. Tom had gone, at midnight, to the Moravian cemetery where, at dawn on Eastern morning, the Moravians would have their sunrise service.

Hundreds of others were already there, waiting for the marvelous music with which the Moravians would greet the first rays of Easter's sun. Midnight was chill with black sky and icy stars. But the air bore the barely perceptible fragrance of the rich Carolina springtime. Tom sat beneath an ancient tree and in the silence of the spring night thought of Grover, and of death, and of life and of his brother Ben with his loving eyes and old man's face.

Tom was jolted from his reverie as the train pulled into Asheville. Arriving at The Old Kentucky Home, he found Ben in one of the larger rooms upstairs. There was a fire in the fireplace, but the windows were opened wide to provide air for Ben. In the corner of the room, Ben lay thin and ashen, gasping out his life, breath by ragged breath.

Fred and Effie were there. Oliver, whimpering with the pain of the great cancer blossoming like an evil flower inside him, had come at last to the "murderous and bloody barn." Mabel and her cousin Effie were carrying out the burden of nursing. Both were exhausted from lack of sleep. Another cousin, Ollie Wolfe, had been a great deal of help. He had stayed with Ben hour after hour, holding his hand, and trying to keep him quiet as the fever-risings brought the constant babbling of delirium.

From a near hysterical Mabel, Tom learned the sequence of events that had led to this terrible moment in his life.

Ben had come from Winston-Salem for his vacation. He had apparently felt well enough until just a day or two before time to return to his job. He began to have chills, and, as his cold progressed and he began to cough, the doctor ordered him to bed, prescribing medicines for him. Julia had been too busy to worry about Ben's bad cold. One of the boarders took care of him, and Mabel came by at least once a day to check on his condition. He had begun to improve, except for a racking, painful cough which got progressively worse.

"I think I have a high temperature, Mabel," he had told her one day. She found a thermometer and read his temperature at 104 degrees.

The doctor returned at Mabel's insistence. This time, he diagnosed the illness as influenza, a disease which had brought death to thousands throughout the country the year before. Now it was at an epidemic stage in Asheville.

"At this point, I got Cousin Effie to help," Mabel told Tom. "She's a good nurse, and she cares more about Ben than anybody else. I'm tired of everything, Baby. I don't know how much longer I can go on. It all falls on me."

When it became apparent that around-the-clock nursing would be required, she and Effie had tried to find other nurses to help. But there were so many people ill that no other nurses could be found. So she and Effie had assumed the full burden.

It was obvious to the doctor that it would be a long, hard pull for Ben. The respiratory ailment which had kept him out of military service had taken its toll. His lungs were in such frail condition that the influenza developed into pneumonia.

It was at that point that Julia sent for Tom.

Now, as Tom watched, Ben's breathing became more and more labored. The doctor had an oxygen tent brought into the room. Each day, Ben's breathing grew more raspy. It seemed to Mabel that neither the doctor nor Effie was doing anything to help Ben.

The conviction grew in direct ratio to her exhaustion.

"Do something," she finally shrieked at the doctor. "For God's sake, do something to help him!"

"Nothing will help him, Mabel," the doctor said quietly. "He's dying."

Julia lay in bed in her room, overcome with grief. Mabel, exhausted by weeks of caring for her father and the recent nursing of Ben on a brutal schedule, fell into a state of collapse. Oliver curled in upon himself, a broken man so stricken by his own pain that the death of his son had no reality for him. Cousin Ollie held Ben's hand, and the doctor smoked a cigarette, swearing softly to himself. Fred and Tom stood watching the face of death.

Before the chill October daybreak, Ben died.

Tom knew that forever he would be haunted by the scornful voice, the bitter laugh, the clumsy affection of his brother, Ben, who had sought but never found the stone, the leaf, the door.

Tom left Asheville shortly afterwards and hurried back into his life at Chapel Hill. This was his junior year and, despite the terrible loss of his favorite brother, he found he could still busy himself and achieve some semblance of normality. He was managing editor of the *Tar Heel*, a position of great responsibility. He was also assistant editor-in-chief of the *Carolina Magazine*. He performed both jobs with distinction. Within a short time, his work as editor of the *Tar Heel* was attracting the attention of newspapermen throughout the state. By graduation time, his reputation was so firmly established that he was offered jobs on several of the state's newspapers.

The *Carolina Magazine* included frequent contributions of poetry and fiction from Tom. Much of it was sentimental and immature, but he was groping surely, if slowly, toward the style which was to be unique in American literature.

Few writers achieve style early. Its development requires the seasoning which only years and experience can give a writer. But Tom was developing it early.

Edwin Greenlaw, one of his teachers, considered Tom an "exceedingly able writer." Greenlaw gave Tom a fine foundation in literature and guided his reading much as Margaret Roberts had done during his high school years. He also helped Tom develop his skill as a writer, encouraging him, leading him, helping him to see his flaws and develop his strengths.

Perhaps even more significant in his development at this stage of his life was the influence of Horace Williams, who taught philosophy. If Tom had a favorite teacher in college, it was Williams. And surely Williams thought of Tom as one of the finest students he had known in his four decades as a teacher. From Williams, Tom learned to question his prejudices, to look at himself honestly, to analyze his thinking, to defy superstition, to reject the superficial.

Another teacher with whom Tom related well was Frederick Koch. Koch had recently arrived from the University of North Dakota, possessed of a vision. Professor Koch knew that throughout the breadth of the land, great drama lay in the tales, legends, and songs of the people. Their dreams, their hopes, fears, and failures were all deposited in folk literature. Koch's dream was to train young dramatists from among the people to write folk plays as an outgrowth of the mass of folk literature. To set about doing this, he organized the Carolina Playmakers, which was humorously called the "Ladies Aid

Society" because its first seven members included six female students and Thomas Wolfe. Its formal title was English 31.

Tom Wolfe's enthusiasm and enormous energy matched Koch's, and the two of them began to recruit. Soon, eleven men had enrolled, among them Paul Green. Green's play, *In Abraham's Bosom*, would one day win a Pulitzer Prize. He wrote two historical dramas—*The Common Glory*, recounting the early days of the Jamestown colony, and *The Lost Colony*, which was about Sir Walter Raleigh's ill-starred venture. These two plays were written for out-of-doors production. They were to set a pattern for outdoor historical dramas which would later become great tourist attractions.

Koch's method was experimental but not planless. The class met without a text, and there were never any lectures on the technique of the drama. Everything was kept on an informal basis with each student following his own course. As a substitute for a text, the students were expected to read those plays which they felt would help them most in their own development.

Each student wrote a play or several plays. He might read scenes to the class for their comments, which were usually positive rather than negative criticisms. When all the plays were written, six were chosen for an "author's reading." At this exciting event, the authors read their entire plays aloud. And, from the six, three were selected for production.

The three plays were produced by the Carolina Playmakers. Tryouts were open to university students, faculty members, and townspeople. It was in every sense a folk theatre, drawing its strength from the people.

Tom was incredibly busy. He was still aching from the death of Ben. But as editor of both the *Tar Heel* and the *Carolina Magazine,* he was driven to a very heavy workload. His grade average remained high even though all his extra activities, including the Carolina Playmakers, required a great deal of time.

Throughout the winter of 1918-1919, Tom grappled with the complexities of dramatic technique. When the Carolina Playmakers raised the curtain on the first performance of their folkplays, one of the three on the bill was Tom's one-act play, *The Return of Buck Gavin*.

Tom's play dealt with a mountaineer who returned to his home after three years as a fugitive. Capture by the sheriff was certain, but Gavin was compelled to return both by his unwillingness to continue in hiding and by his desire to be back among his mountains and his people, even at the risk of capture and conviction for murder.

Tom himself played the title role. In the statement of setting, Tom described the outlaw as "a great, powerfully built fellow . . . he has a strong, heavily lined face covered by a beard . . . piercing black eyes and heavy black hair." Professor Koch saw that Tom fit the part physically; but, more important, he believed that the character of Gavin required an actor who could project intensity. So Tom played the part. His debut as playwright and actor added a new dimension to his character and reputation.

He wrote other plays: *Payment Deferred* and *Concerning Honest Bob* were both published in the *Carolina Magazine*. *The Third Night* was produced by the Playmakers.

Through the study of drama, Tom learned much about the portrayal, motivation, and development of character, as well as scene construction and visual effect. But he never learned that characteristic of drama best described as "economy." One of his editors later said that teaching Thomas Wolfe to write plays was like trying to put a straitjacket on a whale.

But at this period of his life, Tom saw the drama as the door to fame and fortune, both of which he craved as a hungry man craves food. His pursuit of the phantom of fame was almost an

54

obsession with him. The excitement of opening night, the lights and scenery, the crowd of sophisticated people, all held an enormous attraction for him.

In the Playmakers, Tom learned much that was to be of value to him later in life. But his conviction that the drama was his "language" served only to delay for years the beginning of his career as a novelist. It also brought him a series of shattered dreams.

In June, 1920, when he was nineteen years old, Tom was graduated from the University of North Carolina. He had been an exceptional student, both in terms of his academic record and his extracurricular activities.

Julia and Oliver came to Chapel Hill to attend the events of Commencement Week. Oliver was twisted now and weakened by the spores of cancer threading throughout his great frame. He was too weak and in too much pain to attend all the programs. He did not see the actual commencement ceremony at which Tom received his diploma, but he did stand with the crowd to hear his son perform as Class Poet. Tom read his poem under the historic Davie Poplar, where the governor is supposed to have stood to select a site for the university.

Julia saw everything, and she was escorted to the commencement program by a young history teacher who was a friend of Tom's. This teacher, Frank Graham, was later to serve as President of the University of North Carolina, as United States Senator from North Carolina, and as an outstanding mediator for the United Nations.

And so Tom, who had come to Chapel Hill only because he was forced to do so by his father, rounded out his four years with honor. The University of Virginia and Princeton had faded from his memory.

"I hate to leave this place," he wrote to a friend just a month before graduation. "It's the oldest of the state universities, and there's an atmosphere here that's fine and good.

Other universities have larger student bodies and bigger and finer buildings but in the spring there are none, I know, so wonderful by half. I saw old Carolina men home for Christmas who are doing graduate work at Yale, Harvard, and Columbia. It would seem they would forget these old brown buildings in more splendid surroundings, but it is always the same reply: 'there's no place on earth can equal Carolina.' That's why I hate to leave this big, fine place."

But, like all graduates, his sadness was tempered with anticipation and with enthusiasm for the future. The anticipation was, for Tom Wolfe, bright and confident. He was sure that, through his endeavors as a playwright, fame and fortune were not far beyond his certain grasp.

6

I saw the sure destruction of my dreams and my poetry and myself, and I couldn't face it.

Letter to Julia Wolfe

"MERCIFUL GOD!" SHOUTED THE OLD MAN, "Oh, that this should come upon me in my sickness and old age. It's just too cruel. I've given that ungrateful wretch the best education money can buy! I've sent him to the greatest university in the South! He's been offered finer jobs than most boys dream of! I've done all a man could do. I'm sick and old. I'm finished with him."

Tom had just announced to his startled family that he wanted to do graduate work at Harvard. His father's attitude was typical of that of the entire family. They were baffled and angered by what they considered Tom's unreasonable demands.

His career in law had been forgotten for over a year. The family had gradually come to accept the fact that Thomas Wolfe would never become the lawyer-politician his father wished him to be. Tom had never said, "I'm not going to study law." None of his family had said it. It was just a development they had come slowly to accept.

As a result of his work on the *Tar Heel* and the *Carolina Magazine*, journalism seemed a more likely career, and slowly the family had come to think of Tom as a newspaperman. Ben had established newspaper work as a good profession so far as the Wolfes were concerned. And through his work on the Asheville and Winston-Salem papers, he had familiarized them with the world of newspapers. Their interest in journalism was considerably brightened by the offers Tom had had from several newspapers around the state.

Oliver, however, had been more interested in the offer Tom had recently received from the Bingham School, near Asheville. This traditional and conservative military school had offered him a teaching post which promised the income, prestige, and dignity which Oliver had wanted for his youngest child. Tom saw the offer primarily as an opportunity to be near his ailing father. But he viewed it as a dismal future indeed. The school would confine him within a double prison: he would remain walled in by the mountains and by the second and more restrictive wall of the school's sterile military discipline.

He did go out to the school for an interview, however. His family demanded at least that much. He came away firmly set against teaching as a career.

Tom was sustained in his drive toward graduate work at Harvard by three of his teachers, Greenlaw, Williams, and Koch. From Koch's point of view, Harvard's primary attraction was George Pierce Baker, one of the country's leading authorities on the drama. Baker's most important class was formally listed as English 47. It was more popularly known as the 47 Workshop, and it drew Tom irresistibly. It was the country's finest course in the technique of the drama, and Tom saw it as the door to his future.

Tom couldn't remember a time when feelings rose higher in the Wolfe family than they did that summer. The anger seethed just under the surface of all their contacts, breaking into the open more and more frequently. There was bitterness, recrimination, accusation, and counter-accusation. Oliver's attitude was one of self-pity. He had done all a father should do, he felt. And now that he was so terribly ill, he thought it cruel that Tom should torment him about doing more.

59

Mabel was furious. Tom had been given everything she had been denied. And now, when she was working herself into a state of total exhaustion, caring for their dying father, Tom was thinking only of himself.

Julia merely fretted. She wanted Tom to have whatever he wanted and felt he needed. Yet she did not want to quarrel with all the others.

The opposition of the family merely strengthened Tom's resolve. He would go to Harvard. He would enroll in the 47 Workshop. He would become a rich and famous playwright. Let his family talk all it wanted to about writers starving in garrets: he was willing to starve, if that was a requirement. He refused to give up his dream of the theatre.

Late in the summer, Mr. Wolfe's illness became more severe. It became obvious that further radium treatments were necessary, and, in August, Mabel and Fred took him to Baltimore again. But before he left Asheville, Oliver and Julia talked of Tom's future.

"I've done all I can do for him," Oliver said after a long discussion. "My sickness is taking all my money. Oh, it's pitiful. I'll have nothing left to bury me. If you want him to go to Harvard, you'll have to pay his way."

Tom immediately began to press Julia for a favorable decision. Finally, he suggested that he be allowed to go to Harvard for one year, with all costs to be deducted from his portion of his inheritance. To this, Julia apparently agreed, because Tom's application for admission to the Harvard Graduate School in Cambridge, Massachusetts, was approved in mid-September.

At Cambridge, Tom was not, as he had been his first year at Chapel Hill, a "stranger and alone." Professor Koch had written in his behalf to George Pierce Baker. Tom felt that he was known to at least one of his instructors.

Since he was so late in being admitted, Tom found that the

best rooms had been taken. But he did find a room of sorts in the home of a visiting Carolina faculty member who was on leave to do some work at Harvard. The instructor had leased a large old house and had rented several of its rooms to help pay the costs of his graduate study.

Tom viewed with dismay the room available to him: it was an attic room with sharply sloping walls. Tom's rangy figure could stand erect only in the middle part of the room. But he felt fortunate to have found any room at all.

The good part of the living arrangement was the fact that two other former Carolina students were in the house. He had known them both at Chapel Hill and was delighted to find them in Cambridge.

One of the two, William Polk, was a quiet, almost diffident young man who would later become one of the South's outstanding liberal newspapermen. The other was almost his exact opposite. Albert Coates was a hard-driving, aggressive individual. He would, in his later years, be the founder of the University of North Carolina's unique "Institute of Government."

Tom also had relatives in Boston. His uncle, Henry Westall, had for many years been a Unitarian minister. He was, at this time, a real estate broker. Uncle Henry was much like his sister, Julia Westall Wolfe, and Tom spent many happy hours with the Westall family.

Tom's relentless drive to attend Harvard was transformed, once he'd been admitted, into a tremendous drive to succeed. He was not the same Thomas Wolfe who had joined every possible organization in his undergraduate days. At Chapel Hill, Tom had permitted his interests to sprawl into dozens of organizations and activities. At Harvard, he concentrated all his efforts on his classes.

Few American writers have ever been so intent upon achieving their objectives as was Thomas Wolfe. Few have

61

ever so focused all their drive and energy. Tom's intensity of effort began at Harvard. From this time on, he drove himself to the very limits of his endurance, thrusting constantly toward the goals he had set for himself.

He rarely permitted himself a respite from his work. But one of his sources of genuine joy was the Westall family. He visited them frequently on Sundays. There was always much exciting conversation, great bursts of laughter, huge quantities of home-cooked food which he always enjoyed.

Occasionally, he would go out for an evening with Polk or Coates or, occasionally, both. One of their favorite places was Durgin Park, a marvelous restaurant in Boston's wharf and dock district. Tom loved the cobbled streets, wet and shiny, and the boxes of vegetables and iced fish that were stacked everywhere along the streets. He liked the reddish brick buildings, their windows cataracted by greasy-gray dust, their green-painted window frames chipped and flaking. Up the dark stairway of one of these buildings, there were the immense rooms of Durgin Park. There were long tables with red-and-white checked table cloths. From mammoth kitchens came trays heaped with steaming food which Tom attacked with vigor and high good humor.

The 47 Workshop was an exciting experience and Baker a brilliant teacher. Baker's first assignment to his students was that of adapting a short story for theatrical production. Tom's first attempt was a failure: he even had to have one of the characters die of a sudden heart attack in order to follow the plot of the story. But he was sensitive and self-critical enough to know how very bad his adaptation was.

In a second attempt, he departed completely from the story's original plot and "struck a keynote greater than that the short story author thought of." Tom also began work on a one-act play which he thought would be "gold, pure gold."

In a letter to Koch, he wrote that the idea of writing plays had seized him with a "death-like clutch."

"I am reading voraciously in the drama," he wrote, "stocking up with materials the same as a carpenter carries a mouthful of nails. I am studying plays, past and present, and the technique of these plays, emphasis, suspense, clearness, plot, proportion and all the rest. I've come to realize that this doctrine of divine inspiration is as damnable as that of the divine right of kings. Coleridge, certainly one of the most inspired imaginatively of the poets, did more research for the 'Ancient Mariner' than does the average chemist in writing a book."

"For Heaven's sake," he demanded in the same letter, "what do we go to the theatre for? I go to be lifted out and away, and, if that sensation leaves as soon as the curtain falls, I don't think the play is worth a single curse. It's a species of fairyland, I think, this theatre, and I want fairyland to last with me after the players have passed off the stage . . . If a play hasn't some lifting quality besides bare, sordid realism, then it becomes nothing but a photograph of life and what place has a photograph in art?"

As Tom worked on both idea and form, his perception of the drama sharpened into clearer focus. He was groping his way toward the ice-clear vision of the artist and his duty to his talent and to his material. Largely because of this steadily clarifying vision, he had little patience with "the knicker-bockered, golf-stockinged, Norfolk-jacketed" students in the 47 Workshop. He came to detest their mincing criticisms, their posings and posturings, their artificiality. For their part, they looked with ill-concealed scorn upon this stammering, unsophisticated hillbilly with his shaggy hair, dirty shirts and rustic bawdiness.

Tom's vitality began to be sapped by a severe cold he'd come down with on his way from Asheville to Cambridge. "The thing got down into my chest," he wrote to his mother.

"I began to cough—at first a dry cough, then a rattling, tearing sort of cough. . . ."

The coughing became increasingly painful, and soon his right lung was painfully sore. Each time he coughed, there was a stabbing, searing pain in his chest. "One night, I started coughing . . . and I put my handkerchief to my mouth. When I drew it away, there was a tiny spot of blood on it. I was half sick with horror and I tried not to think of it."

Tom applied all sorts of cough remedies and chest rubs. He even swallowed large quantities of ointments. Finally, the cold was cured, the cough went away, the chest pains stopped. But the horror remained: "I saw the sure destruction of my dreams and my poetry and myself and I couldn't face it," he wrote to Julia. "But then, almost in miraculous fashion, I steadied, my mind cleared and the old fear left me."

What he had called fear, Tom now called "fatalism." This was actually whistling in the dark to keep his nerve up. Tom was playing with words, denying fear was fear by giving it another name. Tom never forgot that spot of blood on his handkerchief. It drove him even more furiously to complete as much work as possible before death would destroy him. "I mean," he said, "to express myself to the last ounce."

As Tom had told Koch, his reading was primarily in the drama. But the great Widener Library at Harvard was a steady challenge to his appetite. He raided the library much as a freebooter looted a city in wartime. He would rush into it and rush out again with an armload of books. He would attack them with ferocity, determined somehow to read all the books ever written. Though he himself tended to exaggerate the number of books he read, he surely must have devoured hundreds of them.

Tom was working, by midterm, on two plays for the 47 Workshop. One was *The Mountains* which was in a very real sense autobiographical. Tom could readily identify himself with the main character, a young physician who had returned to practice among his mountain people. Tom found tragedy in the young man's fight against conditions which would inevitably destroy him. In the background, Tom created a living presence: "Those monsters, the mountains, racing like hounds across the horizon, shutting these people eternally from the world, hemming them in, guarding them, and finally killing them."

Another play to which he was applying himself was at various times given different titles. The final title he gave it was *Mannerhouse*. The subject of *Mannerhouse* is the struggle for ownership of the ancestral home of a proud old aristocratic family. The family is represented by an ineffectual man who has little left except the crumbling old house, his own dignity, and the loyalty of an aged Negro servant. Seeking, and ultimately securing, ownership of the house is a "vulgar, coarse and mean, but able, member of the lower class" who has risen to wealth and power.

Tom thought also of trying Asheville itself as the subject for a play. He thought in terms of "a play of a town which never had the ordinary, healthy industrial life a town ought to have, but instead dressed itself up in fine streets and stuck hotels in its hair in order to vamp the tourist populace."

He described a variation of this theme in one of his infrequent letters to his brother, Frank: "There's a good play in the boy who lets the town vamp him, who sees the rich tourists and their mode of life and thinks he must live that way; who gets a job without enthusiasm and ambition in order to pay his way around at night and who finally settles down a dull, plodding, month-to-month fellow till he dies. The town got him. The octopus drew him up. It sucked away his youth, hope, ideals, ambitions and left a clean shirt front. You and I

65

have seen that fellow dozens of times. I believe there's a play there. There's a play in everything that lives if we only had the power to extract it."

Gradually, Tom's promised year at Harvard drew to a close. The fact that he had completed most of the courses required for a master's degree was small consolation. He hadn't completed them all. Nor had he extracted everything he wanted from the 47 Workshop. Yet his mother had promised him only a year and the end of that year was upon him.

He had almost no money. He tried for a job on an ocean liner, but failed to get it. He was homesick and lonely and certain that his family would no longer support him at Harvard. He assumed that he would be expected to return to Asheville, but his mother didn't answer his letters. It was the beginning of the tourist season and she was too busy with her roomers to write to him. He hadn't enough money to pay his rent or to buy food. It was fortunate for him that two elderly ladies were willing to let him have room and board on credit until he could get some money.

Five weeks passed with no word from his mother. Finally he wrote a letter which was a mixture of fear, despair, and melodrama:

"If the time has come for me to go out on my own, so be it," he wrote. "Please try not to treat me with indifference when I am alone and far away. . . . You didn't want me at home: you said nothing about my returning, and I shall see that your desires . . . are satisfied. I am being put out of my room . . . it is leased for next year. I have nowhere to go. I have heard nothing from you. I cannot, will not, write any more [letters]. I am too deeply stirred, too grieved and disillusioned to add anything to what I have written."

7

Come to us, Father, while the winds howl in the darkness
. . . for we are ruined, lost, and broken if you do not come,
and our lives, like rotten chips, are whirled about us on-
ward in darkness to the sea.

Look Homeward, Angel

Tom's humble pleas for money were, at last, effective. During the late summer of 1921, Julia agreed to send Tom back to Harvard for one additional year. That year began with a sense of desperation: Tom felt the icy clutch of failure upon him. He had done well with the courses leading to a degree. But the essential thing was to learn to write plays, and, in that, Tom felt he was making no progress.

His work was marked by constant beginnings and few endings. He wrote by fits and starts, beginning new plays then abandoning them for better ideas. Finally he settled down to work on *The Mountains* on which he felt his whole future rested precariously. He hammered away at it, and finally, in the winter of 1921, it was ready for production.

"It was a complete and dismal failure," he wrote. What had seemed so fine in manuscript was wretched on the stage. For the first time, Tom was uncertain about his future, especially his future as a playwright.

He contemplated the idea of abandoning a writing career. The only avenue open to him now seemed to be teaching. But such a future was unthinkable, because it represented total failure. If he were to be forced into teaching, then he might as well have accepted the position on the faculty of the Bingham School at Asheville, when it had been offered.

The failure of *The Mountains* and the uncertainty about his future plunged Tom into a morbid depression. He brooded about his failure, his lack of talent. He considered dropping out of the 47 Workshop, and he wrote several letters to Baker —letters which he could never bring himself to mail. Each letter told Baker that he wanted to drop the course, and each hinted that Baker had not done as much as he might have to help Tom.

Professor Baker was unaware of Tom's ambivalence since the letters were never mailed. He was unaware of Tom's growing resentment toward him. And he was unaware that Tom was thinking of *The Mountains* as a three-act play rather than its original one act form. He, therefore, kept urging him to work on the play which Tom was calling *The Heirs* and later called *Mannerhouse.*

Baker was sure that *Mannerhouse* would win the coveted Belmont Prize, consisting of an award of five hundred dollars and a guarantee of a New York production. At this point, Baker thought of Tom as an "intelligent, ambitious and well-equipped" young man. He had great faith in Tom's talent, but little confidence in his ability to exert self-discipline. On that matter, Baker saw Tom's future was in Tom's own hands, and his success depended largely upon his ability to discipline himself to the restrictions of the drama.

For his part, Tom felt that Baker was neglecting him. He was convinced that when *The Mountains* proved to be such a bad play, Baker had decided to spend his time and effort on the more promising students. This, of course, was not true, but Tom believed it more firmly each day. He became resentful and sullen. After all, he had defied his entire family to come to Harvard just to study under this man. And now, he felt, just when he needed encouragement more than ever before, Baker was betraying him, rejecting him, laughing at him as he talked with those sophisticated fools in the class.

It was in this mood that he contacted the university's placement office and asked them to find a teaching position for him. He expressed his wish to teach English in a school in the North or the Midwest. Within a few weeks, he was offered an instructorship at Northwestern University. It was a sound offer, but Tom didn't accept it. Neither did he reject it. He merely refused to respond at all.

Days passed. Then a week. Then a month, and Tom still took no decisive action. Emotionally, he was in a state of suspended animation. Then, in mid-June, 1922, he received a telegram which caused him to be on a train within an hour.

Time was running out for his father. The telegram urged him to return to Asheville at once: Oliver was losing his war against cancer.

In New York, between trains, Tom wrote to the placement office, requesting them to write to Northwestern in his behalf to explain the situation to them. Then he was on the train again, looking sadly out the window at the great barns of Pennsylvania, the immense round hills of southwest Virginia, the great, green sweep of the Carolina mountains. It was a long and lonely journey for Tom, reminiscent of his journey from Chapel Hill when Ben was dying.

The train stopped in Morganton, and Tom got off to buy a copy of that morning's edition of the Asheville newspaper. In it, he read the notice of the death of his father.

So the remaining family gathered at The Old Kentucky Home. There Tom sought out Fred who had been home with his father for several days before his death. Fred, who after his naval service had taken a degree from Georgia Tech, had come home to visit and in so doing had eased his father's remaining days.

Fred told Tom he had discovered, on his arrival, that the cancer had taken a shocking toll on his father. Oliver, past seventy, was pale, almost transparent. Each bone seemed visible, covered with transparent skin. The illness had destroyed his vital personality, shattered his confidence. All that remained were the shards of his spirit. He peered from the prison of his pain-shattered body with eyes fiery bright, not from the old anger, but from fear.

One day Fred had teased his father: "Papa, you look awful," Fred had grinned at the old man. "You need a haircut."

"Merciful God, Boy," Oliver smiled feebly, "I wish that was all I needed."

"Maybe a haircut won't make you feel better," Fred had replied, "but it'll sure make you look a lot better. Anyhow, I'm going to take you down to the barbershop."

With the help of a boarder, Fred had carried Oliver down the steps to the sidewalk and had placed him gently in the wheelchair. Down Spruce Street they had gone, the shaggy, thin, old man huddled against pain and death, and his handsome, bright-eyed son pushing the chair.

Oliver's spirits had begun to rise when he saw the familiar square, the fountain, his shop. People stopped to talk to him, pleased to see him. They inqured about his health, and went through the conversational gymnastics one indulges in with the seriously ill. At the barbershop, he was welcomed warmly by the barbers as well as by those who were passing the time of day in the shop. There were firm handshakes, friendly pats on his stooped and bony shoulder, cries of delight from men who hadn't seen him for months. Some of the men, when they left the shop, told others that he was there. Those came by the shop purposely to see him.

When Fred had pushed him home, Oliver looked fresher and happier than he had in months. He had needed a haircut —it had been over two months since he had had one—but it was the pleasure of seeing his old friends again that erased part of the fear in his eyes.

He slept quietly until suppertime. He ate a larger supper

71

than usual, after which he sat up in bed, telling Mabel every detail about his adventurous trip downtown, about the people he had seen, and what each person had said to him. Mabel and Julia, welcoming this chance of blinding themselves to tomorrow, began to believe that he was on his way to recovery.

Two days later, there was a massive hemorrhage. Oliver felt the life suddenly flowing out of him.

Fred quickly had his blood typed for a direct transfusion. It was a clumsy business in those days. It took hours to determine the blood type. Then, since there were no blood banks, the transfusion had to be made directly from donor to recipient. By the time all the necessary tests had been made, it was too late. Oliver was still alive, but no transfusion could have saved him. They tried to make him comfortable as he moved inevitably toward death. It came on June 22.

On June 23, Tom arrived from Cambridge.

It was a long, strange summer for Tom. After his father's funeral, he would have enjoyed going away from Asheville, but there was nowhere to go. So he stayed on at The Old Kentucky Home, working on his play and talking with family and friends. There were long conversations with Fred, with Mabel and her husband, Ralph, and with his mother. Julia caught at least a part of Tom's vision of a future for himself: she agreed that he should return to Harvard for a third year.

There was some difficulty, that summer, centering on meeting the terms of Oliver's will. The will left to each of the children the sum of five thousand dollars, with the residue to go to Julia.

But the cancer had laid waste his estate as well as his body. After all the expenses, including radium treatments at Johns Hopkins, the estate consisted of about eleven thousand dollars.

Since Tom had received the benefits of an education far

beyond what had been provided for his brothers and sisters, he readily agreed that he had, in effect, already received his share of the estate. It seemed to him only reasonable that the estate should be divided equally among the others.

Julia did not think this a fair arrangement. She felt strongly that he should receive a share equal to the others, in addition to what he had already received as education. But Tom finally won out, and he did not receive any money from the estate, nor did he feel any resentment about the decision.

In September, 1922, Tom returned to Cambridge, enthusiastic and confident once more. During the quiet summer in Asheville, he had gained perspective on his life and he approached his third year at Harvard with new ideas, sketches, plots and dreams of a dozen plays. All of them seemed fashioned of the stuff of success.

But his attention centered on one which he called *Niggertown* and which was to consume all his interest for months. Early in the fall, his concept of the play broadened, and he changed the title to *Welcome to Our City*.

The play centers on a municipal reclamation project involving a ghetto of a southern city. The neighborhood includes the fine old house occupied by a Negro physician who refuses to sell it to the reclamation project. As the date for razing approaches, the physician refuses to move out of his house, and his refusal stiffens the resistance of his neighbors. Tempers flare, and there is a race riot in which the physician is killed and most of the houses put to the torch.

If Tom had stayed within the confines of his original idea, he would probably have retained the original title. But his perspective changed as he worked, broadening until the racial aspect of the play was only a minute facet of the whole. The central theme of *Welcome to Our City* is not racial. The central theme is "Greed, greed, greed—deliberate, crafty, motivated—masking under the guise of civic associations for civic betterment."

Tom worked, a man possessed, on what was to become his finest effort in the drama. It had caught him up, and would not let him go. He wrote about the spirit of "boosterism" rampant in the land; he wrote about drives for civic improvement at the expense of the poor; about the deceit that often accompanies change; about the superficialities of the economic spirit of his time.

"The play is not about any problem—least of all the Negro problem," he insisted. "My play is concerned with giving a picture of a certain section of life, a certain civilization, a certain society."

By January, 1923, a rough draft was complete. Baker, by now convinced that Tom could never discipline himself unless forced by external pressure, scheduled the play for production in May. Rehearsals were to begin in April.

Baker was confident about the quality of the play, and he was confident of Tom's ability to keep to the schedule he had set for him. He invited Richard Herndon to Cambridge to see the play, sure that he would award it the Belmont Prize. He kept pushing Tom toward completion.

As the work progressed, Baker began to see that the play was too complex and too long. Staging would be difficult because of the number and nature of scene changes. He began to urge Tom to cut and simplify. Tom worked furiously, much to Baker's gratification. But, almost too late, Baker learned that Tom's furious activity was not cutting and simplifying the play: he was building it up and filling it out, polishing and perfecting it, and, in so doing, lengthening it.

Now Baker was as desperate as Tom was. It was too late in the year to postpone production. Besides, he had invited Herndon, and he did want very much for Tom to win the Belmont Prize. *Welcome to Our City* represented Tom's last chance. As rehearsal date approached dangerously close, it became apparent to Baker that if he wanted the play shortened and simplified, he would have to do it himself. Only a week before rehearsals began, he began the tedious job of reduction of length and simplifying the scene changes.

No thanks to Tom, *Welcome to Our City* went into rehearsals on schedule. This was a particularly painful time for Tom, as it is for any playwright. Up to this point, the characters had existed only within his imagination. Then, suddenly, they were alive, external to himself, moving about the stage, and speaking the lines he had put into their minds. They did not sound as he had imagined them. They did not look as he had thought they would. Worst of all, he could see all his mistakes, and frantically sought ways of correcting them.

The worst agony for Tom, though, came as the actors approached a scene which Baker had cut from the play. At such times, Tom would moan and rock back and forth in his seat. As time for the missing scene came, the moaning would become a loud wail, and the rocking back and forth would become a great leap from his seat. He would lurch toward the exit, shouting and cursing, swearing that he would not return to witness the butchery of his art. Within a few moments, he would be drawn irresistibly back. He would sit, watching the action intently until the next excised scene came up. Then the wailing, moaning departure would be repeated.

The play opened on May 11th. The audience sat, stunned, through more than four hours of ponderous drama. There were seven difficult and complex scene changes which destroyed the pace of the play, shattered its momentum. The action was massive and difficult to follow. There were thirty-one speaking parts in a cast of forty-four.

Welcome to Our City did not receive the Belmont Prize.

Baker urged Tom to re-write the play and submit it to the New York Theatre Guild for consideration for production.

75

Tom had little but contempt for Baker at this point. But he began to work immediately on a revision. However, he made no attempt to further tighten the play or reduce its length, or simplify it or eliminate its clumsy scene changes. Basically, his rewriting consisted almost entirely of restoring the scenes which Baker had cut from the play.

Late in the summer, Tom went to New York, had a clean copy of *Welcome to Our City* typed, and submitted the play to the Theatre Guild. Then he went to Asheville and to South Carolina to visit Effie.

He had no further contact with George Pierce Baker. He was convinced that Baker preferred the more sophisticated student and that he had given him too little guidance. Baker could not live up to the high standards Tom had set for him. It was strange and pathetic that this was true; for Baker was a good man, a good teacher, and a good friend. Few people ever had more confidence in Thomas Wolfe. There was something dark in Tom which demanded the death of the idols he himself created.

In the South again, Tom tried to sort out the pieces, to chart a course for himself. His education had stretched out to seven years. Academically, he had been outstandingly successful. There was a great question in his mind, though, as to whether he had learned anything at all about how to write plays.

He returned to New York in the fall, where he continued to write and to wait impatiently for word from the Theatre Guild. Finally, in December of 1923, the word came: the Guild would not consider producing *Welcome to Our City* in its present form. If Tom could tighten it, shorten it, simplify it, they would be pleased to look at it again.

On January 10, his money almost gone and no prospects for production of his play in sight, Tom wrote the letter which was to set his course firmly for the next six years:

Dear Professor Watt:
I am informed that there will be several vacancies in
the English department at New York University on
the opening of the new term in February . . ."

Thomas Wolfe, who had dreaded teaching almost as much
as he dreaded death, found that Washington Square College
was his only hope of earning enough money to make writing
possible.

8

He took those . . . swarming classes and looted his life clean for them; he bent over them, prayed, sweated, and exhorted like a prophet, a poet and a priest—he poured upon them the whole deposit of his living, feeling, reading, the whole store of poetry, passion and belief.

Of Time and the River

HOMER WATT, Chairman of the English Department of Washington Square College, considered himself fortunate to have secured Thomas Wolfe for his faculty. Tom's letter to Watt had been a model of frankness, which Watt appreciated. Tom called attention in his letter to the fact that he had no teaching experience, that he was more interested in writing plays than in teaching, and that his extraordinary size might well create "an effect on a stranger that is sometimes startling."

To balance Tom's self critical appraisal, there were favorable comments from some of the most highly respected scholars and educators of the time. Horace Williams described Tom as "one of six remarkable students in my thirty years experience." Greenlaw expressed his "extremely high regard for Mr. Wolfe, both as a student and as a man: he is an exceedingly able writer and a man of interesting personality." Koch described him as "a young man of brilliant mind and rare literary talent . . . possessed of unbounded energy and enthusiasm, a hard worker, a man of sterling character."

And so Tom came to his first teaching position with firm recommendations and the confidence of his department head. The agreement called for Wolfe to teach three classes in English composition for two terms beginning in February and ending in September, for which he would be paid $1,800.00.

He rented a room at the Albert Hotel, where he had stayed

before on visits to New York. Though he later wrote of the Albert in unflattering terms, he was actually quite comfortable there. Tom had never paid much attention to his surroundings from an aesthetic point of view, and the Albert, as shabby and frayed as he himself was, seemed attractive enough.

Within a short time, Tom had worked out what appeared to him an ideal arrangement with the clerks at the Albert. Each time he received a check from the university, he gave it to the hotel desk clerks. This paid his rent and part of his meals—he usually had breakfast at the Albert—and then he drew cash from the remainder as he needed it. When he needed money, he asked the clerk for it, and they gave it to him. Sometimes there was no cash in Tom's "account," in which event the clerks loaned money to him from their own pockets. They would recover it when he deposited his next check.

The hotel was only a short walk from Washington Square College, which was a division of New York University. The college was located at the edge of Greenwich Village, near the heart of New York's most densely populated area. It was also near the point of convergence of all the city's subways which made it possible for students from all over the city to attend the college easily. The Village itself provided inexpensive food, lodging, and entertainment for students who lived away from home and could not afford more expensive surroundings.

The students themselves—not the surroundings—gave Washington Square its unusual flavor. Most of them were from low middle income families: second generation Americans who had been taught that in this country education is the key to prosperity and happiness. They had seen, all their lives, the bitter harvest of ignorance. And so they swarmed into Washington Square to wring success from the college itself. Washington Square offered them their one chance to improve their lot.

Tom had known, of course, that teaching would be a drain on his energy, a thief of his time. But it was worse than he had even imagined it would be. He learned to his dismay that, for eight hours of actual classtime, twenty-four hours of preparation were necessary. The grading of compositions turned in by his students swallowed up another twenty-four hours each week. This left Tom a fifty-six hour week of work at the university and hardly any time left for his writing.

He came to class, the first few days, with a case of nervous tension. Every new teacher faces his classes with a mixture of elation, excitement, and fear. The good teacher never totally loses this sensation, even after years of teaching, but he learns to keep a balance between elation and dread.

Tom very quickly caught the intensity of his students: his own drive and energy were matched easily by the drive and energy of the students.

Tom never developed a sense of the world's time, but he came closer to it at Washington Square than at any other period in his life. Though he was rarely late for his classes, being there on time was quite an effort for him. To make the situation even worse, he quarrelled with an elevator operator and thereafter refused to use the elevator. Therefore, almost every day, nearly late when he entered the building, he had to run up the stairs to his fourth floor classroom.

He would stride into class, breathing heavily from the exertion of running up the stairs. His shirt wilted by perspiration, his tie twisted, his suit rumpled, his uncut hair mussed, he would stalk into the room, muttering to himself. He would put his scarred black briefcase on the desk, then look out over the class, grinning nervously.

Tom's height was now six feet six inches, but he was no longer the skinny, awkward boy he'd been at Chapel Hill. His weight at this point stood at 250 pounds. He presented an arresting figure as he stalked back and forth across the front of the classroom talking, reading poetry, waving his arms, and shaking his head. He did not stammer when he was reading, but it was noticeable when he was lecturing. Anytime he talked, he had difficulty in the control of saliva, and, therefore, he constantly dabbed at his mouth with a handkerchief.

Some of the students made fun of Tom. He was sure they laughed at his stammering, at his occasional slobbering, at his size, his clothes, his intensity. But most of the students, though they terrified him, liked and respected Tom.

The good students quickly learned, as do all good students, what sort of teacher they had. In this case, they sensed that this huge, tormented man was a teacher of potential brilliance. Seeking to learn as much as possible in the time allotted to them, they asked questions which he could not answer. He thought they were trying to trap him. They demanded more and more from his lectures, more detailed explanations, more expressions of his opinions. From time to time, when they disagreed with him, they told him so and argued in defense of their points of view. This was not, as Tom thought, because they doubted him or mistrusted him. The truth was that they welcomed the opportunity to sharpen the steel of their minds against his.

And so, as they dug, challenged, probed, twisted, Tom came to fear them, at times to hate them, and to approach his classes with increasing dread. He came, each day, to his classes, fearful that he would be "devoured"—a terror which became an irrationality. He came even to dread the end of each class period, because invariably some of the students would catch him before he could get out the door, and he was more vulnerable when he was not lecturing.

The demands of his students drove him to meticulous preparation for his classes. His own zeal for perfection of expression caused him to spend hours grading compositions. Where other instructors would mark the papers with check marks and underlinings and a grade, Tom wrote criticisms. Each student received from him a long critique, which was frequently longer than the composition itself.

Tom was severe in grading. He expected his students to work as hard as he himself did. Only grades of C or above counted as credits toward graduation, and, at the end of the first semester, thirty out of over one hundred students failed to make C's. Only two of the one hundred earned A's.

The excessive amount of time Tom devoted to his teaching cut deeply into the time available to him for writing. Yet he did write. His disappointment in the Theatre Guild's rejection of *Welcome to Our City* was tempered by what he thought was their confidence in his ability. He told Margaret Roberts that the guild had requested him to shorten the play, to "develop a central plot which would revolve around a small group of central figures." In short, they told him to make revisions which would result in a more nearly conventional play, which was what Baker had urged him to do.

However, Tom abandoned the play. He wrote a long letter to Frederick Day, in which he told of his current work and of his disposition of *Welcome to Our City*: "I was hectored, badgered, driven to such a degree before, during and after the play, by commendation and criticism—none of which agreed —that I am wholeheartedly and completely tired of my first huge opus. I leave it to all the glory of its imperfections. My world has moved. I am writing a better play: I'll have nothing to do with the old."

Tom had taken *Welcome to Our City* to the Provincetown Players, where it stayed for over four months. "I have gone to them repeatedly, pushing my way through the crowd of short-haired women and long-haired men who fill their rooms. . . . Each time, an evil-looking hag with red hair has gone into a little room, shuffled some papers, and returned with the information that the play reader had the play."

84

Days continued to slither by without his having heard from them. Meantime, at least one publisher was moderately interested in publishing the play in book form. Tom was not interested in book publication before stage production.

Another publishing project met with an equally unenthusiastic response from Tom. Professor Koch was ready to publish the second series of *Carolina Folk Plays*, written by the Playmakers, and he wanted very much to include *The Return of Buck Gavin*. Tom did not want to tell Koch that he could not publish the play, but his opposition was clear to almost everyone except Koch himself. In later editions, he requested that the play be omitted. But the first edition included it, and Tom was never comfortable about it. "I'm not ashamed of the play," he wrote to Margaret Roberts. "But I wrote it on a rainy night, when I was seventeen, in three hours."

Tom now was turning his attention to *The House*, originally called *The Heirs*, and finally titled *Mannerhouse*. The play was begun in the 47 Workshop, and now he began to focus his attention on it again.

"The desire to write has, for the first time, become almost a crude animal appetite," he wrote at this time. "And this is because of the obstacles thrown in the path of creation. During the few hours left to me, I write like a fiend on one of the finest plays you ever saw."

This play, *Mannerhouse*, is set immediately before and after the Civil War. A brief prologue, set in Colonial times, shows an ancestor of the main family in the play—the Ramseys—building a great house with slave labor. It is more than just a house he is building: it is a kingdom inherent in the house, and he and his descendants will be the kingdom's rulers. "My house will be more strong than death," Ramsey says. "It will possess and make its own the lives of valiant men and women when I and my sons are gone . . ."

From this Colonial prologue, the play moves directly into the Civil War. Another Ramsey, a Confederate general, is ready to move his army into the field. There is a grand party in his great house, during the course of which there is much drinking, much gallant swaggering, much boasting about the prowess of the southern soldier . . . the aristocratic soldier, not the rabble.

The general's son, Eugene Ramsey, is the only one who sees the enormous folly of the impending war toward which the guests are ready to ride so confidently. The others are certain that the war will be terminated within a few weeks as a result of Yankee cowardice pitted against Confederate courage. One character says, "Snap your fingers at them and they will run like rabbits."

To which a ghostly voice replies: "Then snap your fingers, gentlemen. Snap your fingers!"

Eugene is cynical about the probable outcome of the war and about the motivation of the men. In one scene he mercilessly baits a young aristocrat, leading him to say all sorts of sentimental and adolescent things about the sort of sash he will wear at his waist and the plume he will wear in his hat. Sashes and plumes are all he can see of the war.

Another conflict centers on Porter, a semiliterate man who comes to Mannerhouse to protest the conscription of his son. He makes no mention of love for the boy, or fear that he will be killed. His primary concern was the harvesting of his crops. He needs the boy to help him on the farm. Porter, whose face is "narrow, small, mean and pinched," looks upon the impending conflict as a rich man's adventure and a poor man's economic disaster.

The general, with fine contempt, gives Porter title to a tract of land in payment for his son's services. Porter accepts it and leaves the house, a contemptible man from the point of view of the aristocratic Ramseys.

As the time comes to leave, Eugene clarifies his attitude toward the war. He tells his astonished father that he is going to war because he respects him, not the mythical Southern manner or the Southern cause.

At the end of the war, the men return. Eugene, who was the only one who believed that the South would be destroyed, is now the only one who can comprehend the reality of its destruction. The others pretend that it never really happened. One of them says that they were defeated, not beaten. Eugene cannot accept this spurious comfort, but he cannot deny it to them.

All the servants are gone from the great house, except the giant, Tod. General Ramsey and the others cannot understand the Negro slaves having chosen to be free. The general's health and his wealth have been shattered by the war, and understanding is now beyond his feeble grasp.

The semiliterate Porter replaces Ramsey as the man of wealth, influence, and power. He has, all through the years of the war, used the land he was given to build a fortune. He has none of the grace and manner of his predecessor. But he does have the power. Ultimately, he comes into possession of Mannerhouse.

Eugene, disguised as a workman, comes to work on the house. Porter, who wants it as a symbol of the new power which has become his, plans to spend a large sum of money restoring the damage caused by years of neglect. Eugene is accompanied by Tod, the giant Negro. Tod finds the columns which support the entire structure weakened by age, just as the old society of the South was weak. He manages to tear the columns down, much like a Biblical Samson, and the whole house comes down with a roar, killing both Tod and Eugene. As the noise of the collapse fades, one hears the ghostly voice say, "Snap your fingers, gentlemen!"

It was this play, begun in 1920, to which Tom devoted his

efforts during the summer of 1924. It was a typically dreadful New York summer, hot and humid. Through the miserable heat, Tom continued to plunge into his classes, larger this session, and to grapple with the minds of his students.

The summer was brightened considerably by the ripening of an acquaintance into a friendship. Olin Dows, whom Tom had known slightly at Harvard, wrote to Tom to ask if he would help him find a room in New York. When Dows, three years younger than Tom, came to New York, they became friends almost immediately. Dows had admired Wolfe intensely at Harvard and was delighted to expand the acquaintance in New York.

Tom learned, with some surprise, that Dows was a member of a wealthy family. Dows' father came to the city occasionally, and Tom wrote to his mother that Mr. Dows took Olin and himself out "to expensive restaurants and the theatre." Olin frequently spent weekends at home, and, in July, he asked Tom to go home with him.

Tom was not a social climber, but he was impressed by the Dows' estate at Rhinebeck, New York. Near the estates of the Roosevelts, the Delanos, and the Astors, the Dows' estate sprawled over two thousand acres. It had a huge house and a gatekeeper's lodge. Dows liked Tom, and he was welcomed at the Rhinebeck estate frequently during all the years he taught at Washington Square.

As the summer ground on, the heat and the classes became increasingly oppressive.

"I have become like some mad beast who sees through famished eyes a pool of forest water," he wrote to his mother. "I have only one thought in mind: to get away—anywhere, anywhere out of this world about me—and finish my beautiful play."

"Anywhere" for Tom was Europe.

9

Yes, the place to work was Paris; it was Italy and Capri
and Majorca. But, Great God, it was also Keokuk and
Portland, Maine and Yancey County, North Carolina,
and wherever we might be if work was there within us at
the time. The way to discover one's own country is to
leave it; the way to find America is to find it in one's
heart.

The Story of a Novel

On October 25, 1924, the *Lancastria* cleared New York Harbor, bound for England. Among the ninety-six passengers was Thomas Wolfe, beginning the first of seven trips to Europe, searching for himself, for his father, for America.

He had met his last class on September 5 and had given his last examination on September 12. He had filed his grades and was ready for his journey. Just a short time before he had written to his mother, charging her with unconcern for his welfare.

"If I should die here, you'd forget me in two months," he wrote. "You will say you wouldn't but you would. I'm not bitter. Only I know you've for the most part forgotten me. . . . You don't know me, Mama. I'm not important to you. I've become a man and you'll never realize I'm older than I was when you took me around with you when I was eight. . . . I shall be great—if I do not die too soon—and you will be known as my mother. There is no one like me, and I shall conquer."

Tom's mood brightened somewhat at the end of the summer. His students, against whom he had raged for weeks, presented him with an expensive pipe. The gesture delighted him and he became sentimental about the people in his classes. But the sentimentality had begun only when the semester was almost over and he knew that he had only a few more days of classes.

He had made a visit to Asheville and persuaded his mother to help him financially with the trip to Europe. He would try to avoid asking her for money. Living costs in Europe would be low, and he had saved some money from his salary. He went into some detail about his expenditures, justifying carefully the purchase of an additional suitcase.

And now, the summer was gone, and the "maddened beast," the neglected and forgotten child of summer, was bound for Europe on a huge liner. Tom investigated it thoroughly. He examined its decks, its highly polished brass, deep-shiny woods. He wandered the labyrinth of its corridors, poked his way deep into its bowels where the great engines pounded. He was impressed especially with the huge gleaming galley.

Since the passenger list was small, Tom became acquainted with almost all the passengers. One especially interesting shipboard acquaintance was with Hugh Tenant, member of a prominent English family who was returning home after five years with the British Embassy in Washington. Another was an elderly couple who had been attending a Rotary convention. He was mayor of a small English town and cordially invited Tom to be a guest in their home during his visit to England.

Tom had planned to spend much of his time aboard ship working. His intention was to write 1500 words a day. He actually did a great deal of writing, some of it on *Mannerhouse* but most of it on a journal of his impressions of the voyage.

On the night of November 10, Tom rushed up on deck when he learned that the beacon lights of England could be seen. He braced himself against the heavy winds and watched the beacons through the dark sea night. The following morning at six o'clock, he stood at the rail looking at "the smooth, round green hills" that rose beyond Plymouth.

Tom stayed in London almost three weeks. He loved it the

moment he saw it, and all his life he was to remember "the familiar smoked brick and cream-yellow-plaster look of London houses . . . and . . . the great dull roar of London, the gold, yellow, foggy light you have there in October." Day after delightful day, he wandered the web of its streets seeing all the places he had read and dreamed of.

From London, he went to Bath and saw the ancient Roman ruins. Then to Bristol. Then—Paris!

Never had there been a place like Paris in the twenties! Artists, painters, poets, novelists, musicians all made their way to Paris. Here the new renaissance would begin. Here were cheap flats, freedom, sidewalk cafes, bookstalls . . . this was the city for the artist: the place where work was done and dreams realized.

When Tom got off the Paris train, he found a hotel near the station. He found the room he rented there to be pleasant but relatively expensive. Tom's intention was to live on a very limited budget in order to minimize the need for dependence upon his mother. He therefore used the room as a base of operations while he looked for a cheaper place to live.

He found the place he wanted in the Latin Quarter. It was a dull, nondescript room five flights up. Though it was somewhat inaccessible and more than somewhat drab, it had the virtue of being very cheap. Tom took the room and told the hotel proprietor that he was going to the theater and would return later in the evening with his baggage.

After the play, he went back to the hotel near the station, got his three bags, and took a taxi back to the Latin Quarter. It was well past midnight by this point, and the hotel was locked.

Tom pounded on the door and rang the bell until he awakened the porter, who let him in. There was some doubt in the porter's mind that this huge American actually was entitled to a room. But Tom finally convinced him. The porter, sleepy and out of sorts, was ready to carry Tom's luggage to his room when he discovered it was five flights up.

He immediately began to limp, hobble, wince, point to his leg and speak in a slight whimper. He finally made Tom understand that he was a wounded veteran of the war and that to carry his bags up flight after flight of stairs was beyond his limited strength.

Tom agreed to carry the two smaller bags himself. The porter would arrange, in the morning, to have the larger bag sent up to his room. There was an exchange of goodnights, and Tom climbed wearily to his room for his first night's sleep in the Latin Quarter.

Next morning, when Tom came downstairs, the proprietor was on duty again. The porter, he told Tom, was gone, but would be back in the afternoon. The big suitcase was nowhere in sight, and Tom assumed the porter had put it in a safe place.

He spent most of the day sightseeing. In the afternoon, he returned to his hotel and found that the porter had also returned and was engaged in an excited conversation with the proprietor who was obviously upset.

Tom learned, to his dismay, that his bag had been stolen. Another man, the porter had insisted, awakened him after Tom went to his room. The man had come to inquire about a former guest of the hotel. He must have taken Tom's bag with him when he left.

Tom was beside himself with anger. The bag had contained a few items of clothing—socks and underwear—and the only copy of *Mannerhouse*.

A heated argument began. Soon the proprietor's wife heard the disturbance and hurried to join in. Everyone talked at once, gesturing wildly in an attempt to bridge the language barrier.

As the argument became increasingly futile, Tom left the

hotel. The three Frenchmen were still arguing. He went directly to the police station. The police were concerned and attentive. They took down a detailed description of the bag and its contents. They told Tom how sorry they were, but there was nothing they could do. Tom protested and they shrugged as only the Paris police can shrug.

Tom considered pressing suit for damages, but learned that under French law he would be able to secure no more than five hundred francs without an expensive superior court trial which he would probably not win.

Tom went back to the hotel. He found that the argument had ended. All was quiet and serene. The proprietor had an expression of quiet, superior triumph on his face. He calmly announced to a startled Tom that the hotel was very carefully considering suing Thomas Wolfe for attempted extortion. It was obvious that the second man was an accomplice in the scheme. He had taken the suitcase, Tom would sue, and then the two of them would divide the money: this was the proprietor's version of what had happened.

Tom was enraged but helpless. He agreed to accept the five hundred francs the proprietor would give him. He signed a document releasing the hotel from any further liability and moved out of the hotel.

As soon as he was settled in another hotel, Tom began the enormous task of rewriting *Mannerhouse* from memory. The rewriting kept him busy through December, but he thought the rewritten play was better than the lost original.

Christmas came, and Tom spent a lonely holiday thinking of his family gathered in Asheville. Then, on New Year's Eve, he experienced that most wonderful of moments: meeting an old friend in a strange country. Kenneth Raisbeck, George Pierce Baker's assistant, was in Europe for a year. He and Tom immediately made plans for a gala New Year's Eve.

Raisbeck introduced Tom to two girls from Boston and the

four of them made the rounds of Paris. They avoided the bright, expensive places which catered to American tourists. Instead, they went to little-known restaurants frequented by workingmen and students. All in all it was a fine evening.

Tom found the younger of the two women attractive and interesting. The following week, they spent hours together, exploring Paris. They explored its narrow back streets which tourists rarely see, its cafes, bookstalls, cathedrals. They went to Rheims to see the great cathedral and to Versailles. The four Americans made plans to rent a touring car and visit the south of France together.

Tom had fallen in love with the girl, and was eager to spend as much time with her as possible. He wrote to his mother, told her of his plans, and asked for money to help finance the trip.

But as the time of departure approached, his interest diminished. The girl was alternately too possessive and too distant. She would suddenly become extraordinarily attentive to Raisbeck, which would cause Tom to burn with jealousy. Raisbeck, for his part, became more trying with his bored sophistication, with his constant criticism of Americans.

Finally, Tom withdrew from the plans made by the four of them and quietly made plans to visit the South on his own. He discovered, however, that he had spent far too much money on the girl and had too little to travel. He waited impatiently for his mother to send the money he had asked for.

Then, he received a letter from Fred, telling him that Mabel had been seriously ill and had undergone surgery. The real purpose of the letter, though, was to suggest to Tom the possibility that he had seen all he needed to see of Europe. Perhaps the time had come, Fred hinted, for Tom to stop spending his mother's money and to come home and assume some responsibilities.

Tom wrote to Fred to try to explain to him his reasons for

wanting to remain in Europe as long as possible. This represented his last opportunity to do creative work before he returned to the abrasive routine of teaching which "sometimes kills, or injures badly, creative talent."

As much as he dreaded a return to Washington Square, however, he had agreed to resume teaching in September. Professor Watt had urged him to come home and continue his teaching career, and he had resignedly agreed. But September was several months away; there was still much to see and time in which to see it.

In early February, he received a check from his mother, and used it for a trip to Chartres. From there, he went south to Lyon, Avignon, and Marseilles. By March, he had reached his destination: Saint Raphael. This town of perhaps 6,000 inhabitants was on the Riviera, only a short distance from Nice and Monte Carlo. Tom loved its cream colored houses with their red-tiled roofs, the bright blue of the sky, and the gray mountains that slipped down toward the sea. But time was moving by too fast, and Tom did not stay in Saint Raphael as long as he would have liked. He hurried on to the north of Italy: Genoa, Milan, and Venice.

"I look forward to my return to England," he wrote. "I have loved London ever since I first saw it. And somehow, cold and insolent as they sometimes are, I believe in the character and honesty of the English."

His opinion of the French was not so high. "The French have some very attractive qualities, but I do not trust the depths of their feelings or the honesty of their friendships. There is something false about their amiability."

He disliked the French attitude toward Americans: "American vulgarity . . . is a source of much satire and jest. . . . I suppose like all nations, we have our vulgarities; but I have seen no group of people more vulgar in its manners, its speech and the tone of its voices than the French middle class."

By June, Tom was back in London. He took an extended trip into the lake country, and by mid-August was ready to return to New York. Another brutal year at Washington Square lay ahead of him, and it was with much reluctance that he boarded the *Olympic* for the return voyage.

The *Olympic* crossed the English Channel and put into the port at Cherbourg to take on passengers for New York. Tom stood at the rail and watched the passengers saying goodbye to friends, worrying over baggage, and walking up the gangplank.

He could not know that one of these strangers would, more than any other person outside his family, shape his dreams and change the course of his life.

10

All the passion of my heart and of my life I am pouring into this book—it will swarm with life, be peopled by a city.

Letter to Margaret Roberts

THE OCEAN TRIP WAS UNEVENTFUL for Tom until the ship reached New York. At that time he met a fellow passenger, Aline Bernstein, a woman who had spent her life in the theatre. The daughter of a well-known Shakespearean actor, Joseph Frankau, she had absorbed the special quality of the theatre since childhood. She had an extraordinarily well-developed sense of line and color, and it was little more than natural that she should have become a designer of theatrical scenery and costumes.

Mrs. Bernstein was a brisk, vigorous woman who could give herself totally to her work. She had the ability to see directly into the heart of any problem, to set a clearly defined objective, and to drive toward its achievement with intensely focused energy. Tom later wrote to Henry Carleton that she had "the grit, determination and executive ability that men are mistakenly supposed to have."

To Mabel, he wrote that most people who acquire wealth are unhappy because they do not have "the intelligence or talent of Mrs. B who saw long ago that there's no joy in life unless we can find work we love and are fitted for. She works like a Trojan in the theatre," he continued, "and has made a fine reputation for herself solely through her own ability."

But Aline Bernstein was far more than a hard-driving wom-

100

an who had achieved success through hard work. She was also a woman of vivid personality and physical beauty. If her character was based on her commitment to her work, her personality was rooted deep in love of beauty and zest for life. She found her world a lovely, exciting one, filled with joy. She was a reflection of the wonder and loveliness she saw all around her. And, through a sincere love for people, she drew to her everyone she met. All who knew her were eager to warm themselves at the fire of her humor and generous spirit.

And so it was with Thomas Wolfe. He found himself irresistibly drawn to this remarkable woman he had met so casually on the boat. He was aware of the barriers between them: she was nineteen years older than he. She was married to a highly successful businessman. She moved in social circles almost completely outside the range of his experience. Yet her vitality, her "flower-face," her intense interest in his writing, her unrestrained love for all that was good and beautiful—these called to him as surely as if a voice had called from the depths of his own soul.

But this relationship was to develop into a meaningful one only after Tom returned from Asheville where he went shortly after he had landed in New York. In Asheville, that fall of 1925, he was both amazed and disturbed by the madness he found. The town had plunged into the insanity of a real estate boom, and the land was owned by one man one day and by another the next, and by two or three others before the week had gone. Everybody in town seemed to be making millions in deals for this piece of land or that one; but Tom was convinced that the day would inevitably arrive when "someone calls for a dollar in cold cash and things blow up."

"Boom" prices have always been based upon an inflated demand for land, not upon the intrinsic worth of the land itself. The day always comes when the demand decelerates and prices plunge downward, leaving the owners with plots of ground worth two or three hundred dollars, though they had paid two or three thousand.

Until that day arrived, however, Asheville was a boom town. Promoters rented buildings, provided lavish entertainments, beat the drums of promotion. Property changed hands constantly, and prices soared. Lots were selling for ten times their actual value.

Tom found that Julia, Fred, Mabel and Ralph were not only engaged in the Asheville land speculation but also in the gaudy nightmare of the Florida land boom. He discovered that they could discuss nothing but real estate. He was alternately bored and frightened by it, but he took some joy in seeing people so happy in their present and so confident of their future.

More than any of the others, Julia was wholly absorbed in the land speculation. When the talk veered toward the subject, as it inevitably did, her eyes brightened, her speech quickened and she was sure that one day her land purchases would be worth millions. Tom saw clearly, for the first time, the consequences of his mother's highly developed acquisitive instinct.

Tom admitted that he had benefited, more than any of his family, from Julia's money. But he felt that he had used it to buy something of immense value: freedom to create something beautiful for the world. Julia used the money only to make more money, depriving herself of many of life's joys in order to do it.

As long as he could remember, Julia had been a nag about money. She constantly indulged in what was known in the South as "poor-mouth"—talking as though she were poor when she in fact was not. She constantly reminded Tom of their poverty. She belittled him for any extravagance. This became increasingly annoying to Tom, and it became almost unbearable later when he was driving himself in an almost inhuman fashion. She would make him furious by saying, "Tom's the only one in the family who can make money just writing stories."

Though Tom dreaded another year of teaching, he was glad to return to New York, if only to get away from Asheville. Before he left, he dourly predicted that the bottom would fall out of all the grand land schemes in which his family was indulging. His prediction was to come true the next year. Meanwhile, he could find no solace in his family. Now, more than anything else, he wanted to be with Aline Bernstein. He had described her to his mother as "a very beautiful and wealthy lady who was extremely kind to me on the boat."

He began seeing Mrs. Bernstein with increasing frequency. Tom knew that this could break his heart; yet when Margaret Roberts, one of the few people in whom he could confide, pointed this out to him, he became belligerent and angry. He was disappointed that she did not understand and approve his friendship with Aline.

"If you see only future unhappiness for me," he replied to a warning from her, "what should unhappiness mean to me who called for wine and was given the sponge, and whose bread as a child was soaked in his grief? Am I so rich that I can strike love in the face and drive away the only comfort, security and repose I have ever known?"

Tom clung to Aline fiercely. He became jealous of anyone who showed her even the slightest kindness. He worried about her when he was not with her. This was one source of happiness in his life which he did not dare lose.

The happiness he found in her overflowed into the other compartments of his life. He was happier as a teacher, though part of this happiness was due to the fact that he was a more experienced teacher, more certain of his ability, more familiar with his surroundings.

He still had hopes for the production of his plays. Early in

103

Mr. and Mrs. W. O. Wolfe, 1900.

Wolfe Monument Shop prior to 1900. The tall man toward the center is
Thomas Wolfe's father.

October, he sent *Mannerhouse* to the Theatre Guild. They kept it for weeks and gave it a careful reading before rejecting it. In January, 1926, he sent it to the Neighborhood Theatre, which also rejected it after a long delay.

Aline Bernstein, with her broad extensive knowledge of the theatre, began to discuss his future with him. Tom had known for years that he wanted to write, that he wanted fame. And for almost a decade, he had assumed that he could satisfy his hunger for writing and his thirst for recognition through the theatre. Now, in the spring of 1926, Aline began to lead him carefully toward what would, without her help, have been a shattering decision: to abandon his idea of a career as a playwright.

Aline knew the difficulty Tom would encounter in making a decision to abandon all he had spent so much of himself for. But she knew also that the drama was only one channel, and not the best channel, for the expression of Tom's artistic drive. Tom trusted her loyalty to him as he had trusted no person before. And he respected her judgment. Because of all this, she could help him close the door that would lead him down a long corridor to nowhere and to open a door that would reveal a new dimension of writing which he had never explored.

Throughout the spring, they talked about his future, his dreams, his concept of the role of the artist and his responsibility to his craft. And with each such discussion, Aline's respect for Tom's ability, insight, and integrity grew.

When the second semester ended, Tom had another paid vacation available to him and, on June 23rd, sailed again for Europe.

He stayed in Paris almost two weeks, then went to England. It was there that he began writing a novel which he called *The Building of a Wall*. Like many of the plays he had written, this novel was to have several titles before the writing was completed. His final choice of a title was *O, Lost*, and it was under this title that he later submitted the manuscript to a publisher.

At first, Tom jotted down the various things he wanted to include in the book. He wrote down incidents he remembered from his childhood and his youth. These random jottings gradually were shaped into an outline. Aline bought some large ledgers for him, and in these he began the actual writing of the novel.

Tom rented two rooms—a bedroom and a sitting room—at No. 32 Wellington Square. The house was owned by an ancient man who had been a butler. Tom quickly settled into a daily routine which began when the old man brought him a cup of tea and the morning paper. He would enjoy the tea and read the paper, then shave, dress, and have breakfast. While the landlady cleaned his rooms, Tom would take his morning walk along the Thames.

Returning to his rooms, he would work on the book until noon, at which time he would take a bus to the American Express Company where he received his mail. He would have lunch on Picadilly Circus or Soho Square, then return to work.

The book possessed him and he poured all of himself into it. "All the passion of my heart and of my life I am pouring into this book—it will swarm with life, be peopled by a city," he wrote to Margaret Roberts. "I am telling the story of a powerful creative element trying to work its way toward an essential isolation, a creative solitude, a secret life . . ."

He also indicated to her something of the extent to which he would draw upon his own experience: the book would include "as desperate and bitter a story of a contest between two people as you ever knew—a man and his wife—the one with an inbred . . . instinctive terror and hatred of property; the other with a growing, mounting lust for ownership that is finally tinged with mania—a struggle that ends in decay, death, desolation." This undisguised use of the conflict which

"Old Kentucky Home," Mrs. Wolfe's boarding house. Wolfe family: W. O. Wolfe, Ben, Mrs. Wolfe, Mabel on lawn, and Tom sitting on stone wall. The house still stands much as it was in 1908.

Tom attended the North State Fitting School conducted by Mr. and Mrs. J. M. Roberts. In later years, Tom referred to Mrs. Roberts as "the mother of my spirit."

had characterized and shattered the relationship between his own parents was a portent of what was to come in the remainder of the book.

In September, Tom had reached the point that he felt he needed a vacation, a rest from his work. He took a holiday in Brussels. At one point, he decided upon a sightseeing trip to the site of the Battle of Waterloo. He bought a ticket on a sightseeing bus.

There were only a half dozen or so tourists on the bus when it began its tour, so Tom had an opportunity to observe them all. Among the group was what appeared to be a family: a middle-aged man and his wife, a young man dressed rather sportily, and an attractive girl. When they got off the bus, Tom saw the man clearly for the first time.

The man was, Tom told Aline in a letter, "simply, even shabbily dressed and he was wearing a blind over one eye.... His face was highly colored, slightly concave—his mouth thin, not delicate, but extraordinarily humorous. He had a large, powerful straight nose, redder than his face and somewhat pitted with scars and boils."

The man, Tom was sure, was James Joyce, author of *Ulysses*. Joyce's writing, more than that of any other man of the century, had influenced Tom's.

Tom followed the group into a little cafe where they looked at souvenirs and bought picture post cards. Later, while they were climbing a hill that overlooked the battlefield, Tom asked the younger man if the older one was indeed James Joyce. The young man assured him that he was.

In the cafe again, Tom thought that the young man was going to ask him to join them. He was too shy to permit this to happen, so he quickly took another table and ordered beer. The others had tea, wrote postcards, and talked among themselves in French. Since they looked at him from time to time —Joyce himself stole a glance at Tom two or three times—

Tom was sure the young man was telling them of Tom's questions.

This incident, Tom knew, was all too typical of him. His extreme shyness at times made him stand people off; in this case, his shyness prevented his meeting one of the outstanding novelists of the twentieth century.

In mid-November, he encountered the frustration that plagues every writer: he went "dead and flat." The book had been going along beautifully for weeks, it was flowing well. Then, unexpectedly, he went stale, lost control of his material, groped blindly and helplessly for the tangled thread-ends of his thought. The frustration deepened into fear, fear into despair. He was sure that the novel was finished almost before it had begun. He tried forcing himself to write. He tried diversion. He tried rewriting what he had already written, hoping he would regain the impetus. When nothing was effective, he began to feel the terror which swirls over a writer when he begins to doubt his ability.

His vacation was almost gone; he took one more trip to the continent for a few days, then sailed for New York.

When the boat docked, Aline was waiting for him, excitedly jumping up and down as he walked down the gangplank. Like a child, she could hardly wait to show him her surprise for him: a new place to work. She had rented a huge loft-like garret above a cleaner's shop on East 8th Street. It might at one time have been a sweatshop, but for the remainder of the year, it was to be Tom's home and workshop.

Tom would have the entire floor except for space at one end where Mrs. Bernstein would work from time to time. It had huge skylights which provided excellent lighting. There was only cold water, and the place had no bathtub. But as she had known he would be, Tom was delighted with the place in spite of what he considered very minor inadequacies. Most impor-

Tom, at the extreme left, was about fourteen when this picture was taken. Left to right, Thomas Wolfe, Mrs. Wolfe, Mr. Wolfe, Frank (with his son Dietz sitting on the railing), Mrs. Frank Wolfe, Effie Wolfe Gambrell (with her children), Fred, Mabel and Ben.

Tom Wolfe at fifteen years of age.

tant of all, the unproductive period came to an end, and the writing possessed him once again.

Mrs. Bernstein insisted that he devote full time to the book, and she loaned him money to live on while he wrote. Held tight in the clutch of the book, Tom drove himself furiously, and consumed vast quantities of vile black coffee which, he wrote to Mabel, kept him "alive and cursing."

Professor Watt was disappointed that Tom wouldn't teach, but he did accept the idea, however reluctantly. Tom agreed to resume teaching in the fall semester of 1927, but he reserved the right to change his mind dependent on the course his writing took. Tom was grateful to this remarkable and generous man who had faith and confidence in the basic integrity of the young writer-teacher.

Occasionally, Tom accompanied Mrs. Bernstein to parties attended by the literary and dramatic people whom he basically disliked. He went for many reasons. He liked Mrs. Bernstein, liked being with her, and wanted to do things to please her. Also, the people fascinated him, even while they repelled him. Finally, he desperately wanted to know people in this strange literary world of New York.

Like members of the 47 Workshop, though, Aline's friends seemed to him to be too brittle, too sophisticated, artificial and cruel. Tom described this glamorous segment of society as "a lie of life, false, cynical, scornful, drunk with imagined power and rotten to the core." He almost invariably caused a scene by his belligerence. With careful calculation, he would insult and abuse Aline's friends and goad them into anger.

She was always hurt, baffled, angered by this childish exhibition of his bad manners. She was too well-bred ever to indulge in this sort of behavior. She was too kindly to knowingly hurt or insult anyone, even people she disliked as much as Tom disliked her friends. Gradually, she realized that Tom would continue this sort of behavior. She either had to see her friends less often, or see Tom less frequently. She therefore began to reject many invitations to go out, as well as to accept some invitations without Tom. Then Tom would accuse her of being ashamed of him. Their quarrels were infrequent, but were violent when they occurred.

Tom had already revealed to Margaret Roberts the role his parents would play in his novel. And now, in May of 1927, he revealed more about the web he was weaving. He referred for the first time to her appearance in the "excavation" of his life:

"My book is full of ugliness and terrible pain—and, I think, of great and soaring beauty. In it (will you forgive me?) I have told the story of one of the most beautiful people I have ever known, as it touched my life. I am calling that person Margaret Leonard. I was without a home—a vagabond since I was seven—with two roofs and no home. I moved inward on that house of death and tumult from room to little room, as the boarders came with their dollar a day and their constant rocking on the porch. My overloaded heart was bursting with its packed weight of loneliness and terror. I was strangling, without speech, without articulation, in my own secretions; groping like a blind sea thing with no eyes and a thousand feelers toward light, toward life, toward beauty and order, out of that hell of chaos, greed and cheap ugliness. And then I found her, when else I should have died: you, the mother of my spirit, who fed me with light."

In June, at Olin Dows' invitation, Tom went to Rhinebeck for several weeks. He had been "afraid of the big house and all the swells," but Olin had generously offered him the use of the small lodge for as long as he cared to stay. Tom saw this house as "a little bit of heaven, with a little river, a wooded glade and the sound of water falling over the dam all night."

He prepared some of his own meals, and some were sent to

Thomas Wolfe's play was one of the first produced by the Carolina Playmakers in 1919. Tom shown in the title role of "The Return of Buck Gavin."

Thomas Wolfe in Brooklyn apartment with manuscript
Of Time and the River, 1935.

him from the big house. Almost every evening, he donned his dinner jacket and joined the Dows and their guests for dinner. Tom liked the Dows and he was certain of their affection for him. But he was doubtful of the Dows' acquaintances: "I have a notoriety among them, I believe, as Olin's wild, Bohemian friend."

Tom returned to his teaching in September of 1927. He moved, from the loft on 8th Street, to the second floor of an old house on West 11th Street. He shared the rent with Mrs. Bernstein who also used part of the place for business conferences and for work on her designing.

On his twenty-seventh birthday, Tom wrote a letter to his mother—a strange letter of gentle but clear reproach:

"I have done bad things and cruel things in my wild and lonely life, but on the whole I have lived a decent and honorable life without talking overmuch about decency and honor. I have hated what was cheap, common and vicious. I have loved what was beautiful. I am grateful where gratitude is due, but I confess no obligation to anyone where none exists. It has taken me twenty-seven years to rise above the bitterness and hatred of my childhood. I have no apologies to make for my life, nor any explanations to give to people who cannot understand them. As for you all, I shall continue to remember you and to be loyal to my blood when, as usual, no answer comes to me . . ."

A week later, he wrote to her again to thank her for sending Ben's watch to him. Tom had written to Mabel almost a year before, expressing his regret that the Florida and Asheville real estate boom had collapsed. His mother had written to him several times about the disaster. But as usual she expressed her dismay in such extreme terms that he could not respond to it honestly.

When she wrote to him about her probable future in the poorhouse, he replied that very few people, even those who

118

have nothing at all, die in the gutters. He suggested to her that when people have money to invest, they would do well to "put it in the bank, or on our backs, or in our bellies, where it will do some good" instead of in the pockets of speculators.

The year 1927 ground to an end, and 1928 began. Tom was in a state of depletion: almost all his energy had been poured into his classwork and into the book. There was little reserve to draw on. Yet, final examinations approached pitilessly, as did the necessity of finishing the novel.

On the last day of March, 1928, he wrote to Julia: "I have finished the book on which I have been working the last twenty months a few days ago. In spite of the fact that I know nothing of the book's ultimate fate, I have done a tremendous piece of work. It took over a year and a half of my life, but I did it!"

11

I think the time has come when I must make a bold venture with my life: in some way . . . I want to get the
energy of my life directed toward the thing it desires
most.

Letter to Homer A. Watt

ONCE *O, Lost* WAS COMPLETED, Tom wanted more than anything else to forget it. He was aware of its flaws and weaknesses, but he was unwilling, and perhaps unable, to make the changes necessary to correct them.

One of the major criticisms, he knew, would be of the book's extraordinary length. It was about three times longer than the average novel.

"A revision would shorten it somewhat," he wrote. "But I do not believe any amount of revision would make it a short book. . . . It does not seem to me that the book is overwritten. Whatever comes out of it must come out block by block, not sentence by sentence."

Another target for criticism would be the book's plotlessness. Novels should have clearly defined plots, following an established pattern. Of his own work's form, Tom wrote that "the book may be lacking in plot, but it is not lacking in plan. The plan is rigid and densely woven."

Tom had created a book with "two essential movements, one outward and one downward." In the first, he had shown the efforts of a young person striving for freedom. In the second, he was involved in what he called an "excavation into the buried life of a group of people."

A third criticism which Tom anticipated would be directed

toward the autobiographical nature of the book. "It is obvious that the book is autobiographical," he wrote. "But there is scarcely a scene that has its basis in literal fact. The book is fiction—it is loaded with invention. . . . But it is a fiction that is, I believe, more true than fact—a fiction that grew out of a life completely digested in my spirit. . . ."

By the middle of March, the huge manuscript had been typed in its final form. Tom wanted desperately to have the book read. Yet he feared and dreaded criticism of it. He had worked so long, submerging himself completely in the book, that while he wanted people to see what he had done, he was afraid of adverse reactions. In this uncertain mood, he sent a copy to James Munn, acting dean of Washington Square College.

Wolfe described Munn to Margaret Roberts as "an idealist and a sensitive, romantic person." Munn was "terribly shocked at the pain, the terror, the ugliness and the waste of human life" contained in *O, Lost*. However, he thought it unique and important, and he felt that it should be published without extensive revision.

By April 1, Tom had decided to abandon teaching. "I think the time has come," he wrote to Watt, "when I must make a bold venture with my life: in some way . . . I want to get the energy of my life directed toward the thing it desires most."

In the same letter, he made a final evaluation of himself as teacher, and it was probably a fair one. He felt that he had served the school to the best of his ability. He, who had been notorious for his indifference toward time, had been punctual so far as his classes were concerned. He had been, he thought, extraordinarily faithful in his careful grading and in writing helpful comments on his students' work. But the time had come when it was essential that he commit himself to writing as a means of earning a living.

By late May, he was developing the idea for a second book.

O, Lost had been sent to Boni and Liveright, publishers. After five weeks, he received a notice of rejection: the book was far too long as well as too autobiographical.

He had also given the book to Ernest Boyd, the critic. Boyd felt the book was unpublishable, but his wife, Madeleine, did not agree with him. She thought *O, Lost* was unique and that it would inevitably find a publisher. She had only recently started on plans for a literary agency and she immediately took upon herself the responsibility of finding a publisher, a visionary one, courageous enough to put Tom's book on the market.

She first sent the manuscript to Covici-Friede who rejected it for the same reasons Boni and Liveright had given. But she was confident, not only in her own ability as an agent but also in *O, Lost* and in Tom's future. She continued to take the manuscript from one publisher to another.

Tom went to Asheville for a brief and depressing visit. The enormous real estate bubble had burst, turning the dream of wealth into the nightmare of depression. The people were now as totally absorbed in the bitterness of depression as they had been in the vision of wealth. Tom discovered very quickly that depression was the only topic of conversation. Preoccupied with their economic disaster, which he had predicted, each person he saw told him of the emptiness of loss. Tom very quickly became restless and returned to New York.

He had been planning another trip to Europe. He was eager to sail, but his departure was delayed by the necessity of oral surgery. The work was extensive, costly and extremely painful. And while he waited impatiently for the doctor to finish the work, he wrestled with a decision which had to be made. The J. Walter Thompson agency, one of the country's largest advertising firms, had made him a generous offer. In most ways, he wanted very much to accept it. It would have enabled him to live by his writing ability, which was what he wanted to do. However, the agency insisted that he agree to stay with the firm for at least three years. This he was reluctant to do: he did not want to commit his time to that extent.

So he sailed for Europe with hopes for the publication of his first book, with notes for the second book, and with indecision about the advertising agency position.

After a few weeks in Paris, Tom went to Brussels. He liked its broad avenues and great parks, even though they reflected a French influence which he disliked. He also went to Cologne, Bonn, and Weimar.

At one point, he met James Joyce again. And again, even though they were on the same sightseeing tour, Tom was too shy to introduce himself to this writer whom he admired so much. Tom thought Joyce looked considerably older than he had when he had seen him at Waterloo. But he was more elegantly dressed, and had abandoned his eye patch for dark glasses.

The tour took them to the Frankfort Rathaus, where they were instructed to put large felt slippers over their street shoes to prevent marring the beautifully polished floor. Joyce became preoccupied with the shiny floors and the felt slippers. He discovered that he could slide along the floor with the slippers much as though he were on ice-skates. So while the guide was giving her lecture to the tourists, James Joyce skated about the big room.

The tour also went to Goethe's house, and both Joyce and Tom thought it a lovely building. After a while, Joyce told Tom that he wanted to wander about the old portion of the city.

"Like a fool, I was too awkward and too shy to ask to go along," Tom wrote sadly to Aline. "I'm sure he would have let me. He wanted to be kind and friendly and it would have been a grand thing for me to have gone along with him."

When he had grown tired of Frankfort, Tom went to Munich, primarily because of the "Oktoberfest": the October Fair.

Tom had found German night life "heavy and brutal," centering on food and beer and loud German music. The people ate "great slabs of pork and veal covered with heavy sauces" and "swilled down quarts of beer" and listened to orchestras that "made a terrible noise."

Tom hoped the Oktoberfest would be different. He anticipated a sort of open air market where peasants would sell their wares and dance quaint peasant dances. Instead, he found it to be an extension of what he had already seen. The center of the Oktoberfest was the dark October beer, twice as strong as the ordinary beverage.

He was disappointed to discover that the fair consisted of merry-go-rounds, cheap souvenir stands, sausage shops and dozens of beer halls. "These halls are immense and appalling," he wrote to Aline. They were so crowded "there is hardly room to breathe, to wriggle. A Bavarian band blows out horrible noise and all the time hundreds of people who cannot find seats go shuffling endlessly up and down and around the place. In these places, you come to the heart of Germany; not the heart of its poets and scholars, but its real heart. It is one enormous belly. They eat themselves into a state of bestial stupefaction."

Tom visited the Oktoberfest several times, then sought other diversions. One of his favorite places was a sort of center for Americans. Here one could find a small collection of books which could be borrowed. The center also provided a place for American tourists to meet one another. One day, when Tom went to the center, he found an interesting American couple accompanied by a friend. They were eager to learn as much as they could about Munich, and Tom was as eager as usual to talk.

He told them about the various cathedrals, historic buildings, and museums which were well worth their attention. He also mentioned the Oktoberfest, in which they were interested largely because it was peculiar to Germany. The four of them rather liked one another, the single lady was glad to have his company, so the four of them went to the Oktoberfest.

It was a rainy night, but the weather had little effect on the spirits of the people; the halls were crowded and noisy as they usually were. In one of them, Tom and his friends managed to find a table and to order food and beer. Tom rather quickly grew tired of the other three Americans. After dinner, when they were ready to leave, he quickly told them to go ahead; he would remain for a while.

When his friends had gone, some Germans joined him at his table. He happily joined them in singing loud, spirited stein songs. He left the hall after an hour, but, instead of returning to his room, he went to another hall. He drank more of the strong brown beer and sang until the place was ready to close. Tom was having what seemed to his beer-fuzzed mind a glorious evening. Certainly the Germans loved this great, shaggy giant who could drink stein after stein with them and join in their boisterous singing.

Finally, when groups were breaking up and leaving and members of the band putting away their instruments, Tom decided to leave. Near an exit, he passed a group standing by their table singing one last song. As he passed, one of the men took him by the arm and stopped him. He had probably seen this big American drinking and singing with the others, and simply wanted him to join them. Tom tried to pull away from the man's grasp and move on, but the man's grip tightened. Tom wrenched loose, flung his huge fist in a wide arc, and watched the man lurch backward over a table.

Tom stumbled out into the rain, only to discover that he had gone out a side door into some sort of enclosure from which there was no exit. The rain was pouring down, and the ground under his feet was a slimy, slippery ooze. He turned to go back into the hall to find the proper exit. As he slipped and slid in the mud toward the door, he saw three men walking toward him. One of them was carrying one of the steel-and-wood folding chairs from the hall.

Tom later remembered the next few moments "as a kind of hell of slippery mud and darkness with the rain falling." The first man to reach Tom was hurled away by Tom's smashing fist. The second man swung the folding chair. Tom was unable to ward off the blow of the chair. He staggered and before he could recover his balance, the chair smashed his head again. Then there was a tangle of bodies on him, but he managed to get up even with their combined weight and his uncertain footing. He kept swinging his big fists and, most of the time, felt them connecting. He could not see because of the rain running down into his face.

Fortunately, the police arrived and took them all to the station. Tom discovered that the "rain" that had obscured his vision was blood from severe scalp lacerations inflicted by the chair. After brief questioning, Tom was hurried off to a physician, who hospitalized him.

A mild concussion and several scalp wounds and a shattered nose were bad enough. But added to his pain was his fear of hospitals. He had an irrational terror of hospitals, which had heightened in intensity since the death of his father. Added to pain and terror was his unspoken fear that he might have seriously injured or even killed one of the people who had attacked him.

Sure that difficulty with the police was inevitable, he was eager for release from the hospital. He was certain that if he remained long in Munich he would be arrested for assault. After a few days in the hospital, Tom was released, and, as quickly as possible, he packed and crossed the border into Austria.

By early November, a battered Thomas Wolfe was in Budapest. His face was discolored, his eyes swollen, his nose grotesque. His head had been shaved because of the stitches in his scalp. But at least he was out of Munich.

It was in Budapest that Tom learned of the election of Herbert Hoover as President of the United States. Tom rarely took any interest in politics, and, when he did, his views were ill-informed and immature. He knew little of party platforms. He was not a member of either party, but thought of himself rather vaguely as a Socialist.

The results of this election were especially distressing to him. His dismay stemmed from his conviction that people did not vote for Hoover so much as they voted against Al Smith, and for the wrong reasons. He was baffled by the rejection of Smith who seemed to him the better candidate. He was convinced that one day the people would see their error.

Tom's principal wish now was to be away from Europe. The brawl in Munich had shocked him, frightened him, and disillusioned him. In Budapest, a wave of loneliness and homesickness swept over him. He returned to Vienna, where he found a letter waiting for him:

> "Mrs. Ernest Boyd left with us, some week ago, the manuscript of your novel, *O, Lost*. I do not know whether it would be possible to work out a plan by which it might be worked into a form publishable by us; but I do know that, setting the practical aspects of the matter aside, it is a very remarkable thing and that no editor could read it without being excited by it and filled with admiration by many passages in it . . ."

The letter was signed by Maxwell E. Perkins, senior editor of Charles Scribner's Sons. Although Tom was excited by the interest of such a well known and firmly established publisher, he did not know that Maxwell Perkins was the finest editor of his time. Neither did he know that this letter was an introduction to the best friend he would ever have. As it was, he had no idea that this letter marked the beginning of one of the most remarkable relationships in American literature.

But he made plans to sail for New York in great anticipation. In so doing he was returning home to begin a friendship which would bring him greater joy and deeper sadness than he had ever known.

12

It was as if a sculptor had found a certain kind of clay with which to model. Now a farmer who knew well the neighborhood from which the clay had come might . . . say . . . 'I know the farm from which you got that clay.' But it would be unfair of him to say 'I know the figure, too.'

The Story of a Novel

It would be difficult to find a man more unlike Thomas Wolfe than Maxwell Perkins was. Tom was large and heavy; Perkins was spare and compact. Tom had a tangle of black hair and brooding dark eyes; Perkins was blond with blue eyes. Tom was a sprawling, undisciplined thinker; Perkins was judicious and controlled. Tom always looked untidy; Perkins was always neat, if not elegant. Tom was a volatile, expansive Southerner; Perkins was a predictable, austere New Englander.

But between them, there was the steel of integrity. Both were honest men to begin with. And now they were joined in that work which required the thin, naked integrity of a knife-blade: the production of a book.

They took quick measure of one another on January 2, 1929. Tom had arrived in New York on New Year's Eve. On the first business day of the new year, he appeared in Perkins' small office, nervous and apprehensive. His nervousness was heightened by the way he seemed to fill entirely the small office in which Perkins worked.

Maxwell Perkins, more than most men, was acutely sensitive to others. His business was dealing with writers on their most difficult level. His sensibilities were honed to a fine edge. He saw, of course, that his first job was to put this restless giant at ease. He suggested that Tom take off his coat and sit down. Tom gratefully removed his coat and tugged at his tie and collar until they were loose. They chatted a while about Tom's most recent trip to Europe.

As Tom relaxed, he observed the man on the other side of the desk. Max Perkins looked younger than he was. In his late forties, he looked as though he were only a few years older than Tom. He was wearing his hat: one of his few idiosyncrasies was that of wearing a hat almost constantly. He was looking directly into Tom's eyes, and, about his mouth, there was the trace of a smile. When he spoke to ask a question, his voice was gentle. But beyond the gentleness, Tom could hear the steel. There was no weakness in this man.

Gradually Perkins swung the conversation around to the book. There was a great stack of handwritten notes on his desk. As they began to talk about the book, Perkins referred to these notes occasionally. Tom came to realize that they contained an outline and detailed summary of *O, Lost*.

Perkins' manner changed subtly as they talked. He began to point out strengths and weaknesses, analyzing, evaluating, suggesting possibilities for changes. With an assurance that astonished Tom, Perkins went through the entire book, scene by scene, occasionally referring to his notes.

Perkins' primary concern was with the characteristic which Tom had referred to as "plotlessness but not planlessness." The book was unorthodox in that it lacked unity, at least in the formal sense. However, Perkins believed that with proper deleting and tightening, unity could be built around the family as seen by its youngest member. As Perkins talked, Tom began to see that Scribners' intention was to publish *O, Lost*.

There was another meeting between Tom and Perkins later in the week. At that time, Perkins gave Tom a check for an advance against his royalties. Tom agreed to deliver to Perkins one hundred pages of revised manuscript each week. He later told how, clutching the check, he had left the building and found himself blocks away with no memory at all of walking the long distance.

When Margaret Roberts learned of the acceptance of Tom's

book, she wanted him to receive some sort of recognition immediately. She, therefore, wrote to ask his permission to allow her to nominate him for an award to be given to the citizen of Asheville who had performed the most outstanding service to the community. For the first time, Tom confronted squarely the likelihood that the people of Asheville would not consider his book a service to the community.

"This worries me now that my joy is wearing off," he wrote to her in reply. "This book dredges up from the inwards of people pain, terror, cruelty, ugliness, as well, I think, as beauty, tenderness, mercy. . . ." He told her that he had had no intention of being cruel or tender, ugly or beautiful—that he had, in short, written as he had to write. But in the book, he warned, she would find passages "which will wound and anger people deeply, particularly those at home."

Tom could not bring himself to be more specific. The fact was that he had drawn heavily upon his own experience in writing the book. And his own experience was not separable from the experience of others.

O, Lost was the story of a mountain-rimmed town called Altamont. The family consisted of W. O. Gant and his wife Eliza and their children. Gant was a stonecutter who indulged in flights of rhetoric and vituperation. His wife lived to acquire property. There were several children, including twin boys, Ben and Grover. Grover died in St. Louis where his mother had gone to open a boarding house. Ben died considerably later. Luke was a stammering salesman. Steve was a wastrel. Helen was a volatile, warm, noisy, earthy girl. The youngest son, Eugene, was bent only on getting away. At the end of the book, he has become a student at the state university in the village of Pulpit Hill.

In addition to the Gant family, there was an entire town full of people, portrayed in all their beauty and all their ugliness.

In his novel, the line between fact and fiction was badly blurred. Tom insisted that no artist could use that which he does not have. He must write what he knows, must begin with the use of that which is familiar.

But Thomas Wolfe was not just a diary-keeper or a reporter. He did not merely set down facts as he remembered them. Though he made liberal use of actual people, places and events, they were all changed, shaped, molded by his peculiar vision of life and his fertile imagination. And, of course, there was much in the story which was pure invention.

Tom did not say all this to Margaret Roberts, because it did not occur to him that it needed to be said.

He plunged into the work of keeping his promise to deliver one hundred revised pages each week. And immediately he encountered the problem which had plagued him before and which would trouble him as long as he lived.

"I stare for hours at the manuscript before cutting out a few sentences," he wrote. "I want to rip in blindly and slash, but unless I know where, the result would be disastrous." But Max Perkins did know where, and he helped Tom to see. In frequent and long work sessions, they cut out great slabs of the book, shortening and unifying it.

As had been the case when George Pierce Baker had insisted on cuts in his plays, Tom endured intense agony during each cut. He had known all along that the book was too long and that it would have to be cut block by block. He knew, too, that by cutting out material extraneous to the core of the book, he would achieve a solid unity, a better book. Yet he found the process difficult to bear.

Perkins found a way to make the cutting more bearable: some of the scenes which were removed from the novel, he suggested, might be published as short stories. The first of these was sold to *Scribner's Magazine*. If Tom had been asked to set a price, he would have suggested fifty dollars, perhaps seventy-five. Scribners offered him one hundred fifty dollars. "I almost fell off my chair!" he wrote to Mabel.

This was the first of a number of short stories which were actually scenes cut from his novels. Strangely enough, when Tom tried to write short stories, he was unable to do so. As he had been unable to discipline his talent to the confines of the drama, so he could not force his ideas into the narrow, rigid frame of the short story.

But these scenes from his novels were excellent short stories. The first one, "An Angel on the Porch," was published in the August, 1929, issue of *Scribner's Magazine*. Tom was pleased to have the money from the sale of the story; it was an unexpected bonus. He was also eager to see the story in print.

Although the novel was occupying most of his time, he was teaching two courses at Washington Square, and Dean Munn had offered him a summer teaching assignment and one for the fall semester as well, if he needed the income.

But he had some difficulty balancing his responsibilities as a teacher with those of a writer. He was, for the first time, frequently late in returning compositions which his students had handed in. He would occasionally explain that the delay was caused by the necessity of working on the revision of his novel. He frequently talked to the class about the process of writing and revising the novel. Yet, it appears that he did not neglect his classes: he continued to share with them his enthusiasm and love for good writing.

Tom and Max Perkins were giving much thought to a better title for *O, Lost*. Tom had selected the title from the novel's recurring phrase, "O, lost and by the wind grieved, ghost come back again." Perkins was not pleased with the title, even though it grew out of the book itself. He felt that they should find a title which was both more beautiful and more meaningful.

In John Milton's poem "Lycidas," written as a tribute to a young man who had drowned, there is a line which reads "Look homeward, Angel, now, and melt with ruth." From this line, they selected the phrase which was to be the title under which Tom's first book was published: *Look Homeward, Angel.*

By midsummer, Tom had finished the revisions and was beginning to receive galley proofs for final reading and corrections. He rented a cottage near Ocean Harbor, Maine. A road followed the curving shoreline, and there were cottages with bright tidy flower beds and twisted apple trees with fruit softening toward fall ripeness.

Near his cottage, there was a rickety wharf. Tom gingerly stepped out on it the first time to test its strength under his great weight. It was shaky, but strong enough to support him, and he spent happy hours fishing from it. From the wharf, he could see the small, spruce-forested island in the harbor. At one end of the island, the trees had been cleared away to make room for a small cottage. Tom liked to think of buying it.

In this pleasant setting, he corrected the galley proofs of *Look Homeward, Angel.* In this work, he was assisted by John Hall Wheelock, a Scribners' editor assigned to these final stages of production of the book. Tom had been introduced to Wheelock the day he met Maxwell Perkins, and their friendship grew quickly. But it was never as strong as that which existed between Tom and Perkins.

Late in the summer, Tom wrote to Wheelock about the dedication page for the novel. He had one he especially wanted to use: a quotation from a poem by John Donne. This poem was used, and the book was dedicated to A. B., Aline Bernstein.

"An Angel on the Porch" appeared while Tom was still in Maine. "I had expected convulsions of the earth, falling meteors, suspension of traffic, and a general strike when the story appeared," he wrote. "But nothing happened."

The August issue in which the story appeared also contained a photograph of Tom, a brief notice of his forthcoming book, and a short biographical sketch. It was stated that Tom had received his education at a "small southern college," which distressed some of Tom's Chapel Hill classmates. He asked friends to explain for him that he had not seen the material before it went into print. He would not have referred to the University of North Carolina in any way that would have detracted from it.

"An Angel on the Porch" served as an advance warning to the people of Asheville. Margaret Roberts feared he would cause his family real distress if the short story was indicative of the book that was to come.

"I would do anything to avoid causing anyone pain—except to destroy the fundamental substance of my book," he wrote to her. "I'm afraid, however, that if anyone is distressed by what seemed to me a simple and unoffending story, their feeling when the book comes out will be much stronger."

After a brief visit to Canada, Tom returned to New York, his part of the work on the manuscript finished at last. All he could do was to wait. He was tantalized briefly by the interest shown for his book by the Book of the Month Club. Their interest was mild, and Tom knew that there was very little chance that *Look Homeward, Angel* would actually be chosen. Yet something in him hoped for it.

He was momentarily distracted from his apprehension and nervousness by a visit with an old friend from Chapel Hill, Jonathan Daniels. Daniels was the son of Josephus Daniels, former Secretary of the Navy and publisher of one of North Carolina's most influential newspapers, the Raleigh *News and Observer*.

Tom's friendship with Daniels had begun when they were students at Chapel Hill and would continue until Tom's death. As was true of all his friendships, there was strain, conflict and crisis. But the friendship endured in spite of the stresses imposed upon it.

Tom went home to Asheville in September. There was much interest in his book, some apprehension based on the story in *Scribner's Magazine*. While the story was fiction and was generally recognized as such, there was a disturbing familiarity in character and setting.

Tom tried to prepare his family for what was to come. His warnings were vague and ineffective, however. Mabel came to realize that there was something to fear, but she assumed that Tom had used vulgar language which would shock people. She did not even guess that she and practically everyone she knew would recognize themselves, or think they could, in the novel.

Everything considered, however, the community was excited and pleased about the forthcoming book. The newspaper carried an article about "An Angel on the Porch." George Mc-Coy of the newspaper staff told Tom that the book would be reviewed in the newspaper and on a local radio program.

Tom enjoyed this visit more than most of his trips to Asheville. But he soon returned to New York with a feeling of relief at being away from his family. The conflicts, recriminations, and stresses to which they were compelled to subject one another were more than he could bear for long periods of time.

Finally, in October, 1929, *Look Homeward, Angel*, was published. Several copies, of course, went to Asheville. He had copies sent to his family, to a few friends, and to reviewers. Among them was one in which Tom had written:

> To Margaret Roberts, who was the Mother
> of my Spirit, I present this copy of my
> first book, with hope and with devotion.

13

Young men sometimes believe in the existence of heroic figures stronger and wiser than themselves to whom they can turn for an answer to all their vexation and grief. You are for me such a figure: you are one of the rocks to which my life is anchored.

Letter to Maxwell Perkins

THE PUBLICATION OF HIS FIRST BOOK is an enormous experience for a serious writer. He has laid bare a part of himself—perhaps the most significant part—for all men to see and to judge. From their judgment there is no appeal. All his dreams, hopes, fears, ambitions, center in the book. In a very real sense, he has become his book. Any judgment passed upon it is a judgment passed upon himself.

He waits for the reviews in fear and longing. More than anything else, he wants the book to be welcomed, to be taken freely and without reservation into the minds and experiences of the people.

Every writer wants his book to be accepted by those nearest to him—in Tom's case, his family and Asheville in general.

In Asheville, the shocked silence was followed by an outcry of baffled rage: Tom had dealt mercilessly with them, they thought, and with his family. They had all been exposed naked to the world, in all their pettiness, cruelty and greed—and in all their beauty, love and clumsy tenderness. They saw themselves in *Look Homeward, Angel* as weak and ugly. Tom saw them in grandeur; for to him, even man's flaws were glorious.

Tom clung to Perkins' "prophecy" made a few days before publication: "All I know," Perkins had said, "they cannot let it go, they cannot ignore it. The book will find its way."

One of the earliest reviews was in the October 20th issue of the Raleigh *News and Observer*. It was written by Tom's friend, Jonathan Daniels, and it wounded Tom deeply. "Here is a young man," Daniels wrote, "hurt by something he loved, turning in his sensitive fury and spitting upon that thing. In *Look Homeward, Angel*, North Carolina and the South have been spat upon."

On Saturday the New York *World* carried a review by Harry Hanson. Hanson said that there was some beauty in the book. But, on the whole, it was an unfavorable review. Hanson amused himself, and one supposes, his readers, by ridiculing the book. He especially enjoyed making fun of Tom's style.

Tom was crushed and frightened. The two most important New York reviews would be those of the *Times* and the *Herald Tribune*. He was terrified, certain that those influential papers would follow Hanson's lead.

The *Times'* review, written by Margaret Wallace, came out the day after Hanson's. Unlike him, she saw in *Look Homeward, Angel* an abundance of "drive and vigor, profound originality, rich and variant color." She praised Tom's ability to reveal "facets of observation and depths of reality hitherto unsuspected." She called attention to his "sprawling, fecund, subtly rhythmic and amazingly vital style." She closed her review with a statement of her conviction that this novel should "be savored and re-read, and that the final decision upon it . . . rests with another generation than ours."

One week later, Margery Latimer's review was published in the New York *Herald-Tribune*. "Mr. Wolfe makes you experience a family through twenty years of its existence," she wrote. "He gives you the disharmony, the joy, the hideous wastefulness and the needless suffering, yet not once do you dare shrink from life and not once are you plastered with resentment and loathing for reality and experience. If I could create now one magic word that would make everyone want

143

to read the book, I would write it down and be utterly satisfied."

A first novel does not usually elicit such praise from reviewers of such influential newspapers. Neither of these women ex-
hibited the caution reserved for first novelists; each stated un-
equivocally her belief that *Look Homeward, Angel* was a significant contribution to American literature. The support
given by these two reviews did much to sustain sales of the
book during the first critical weeks after publication.

Sales began to climb. Perkins' confidence increased, and he
ordered a second printing in anticipation of rising demand for
the book. Reviews began to appear in periodicals. The reviewer for the *New Republic* referred to Tom's "literary ability
and . . . scholarly background." *The Bookman* commented on
the novel's "positive grappling with life." Carl van Doren
wrote, "Mr. Wolfe, with much that is heroic in his constitu-
tion, has had the courage of his heroism." Van Doren's review
pleased Tom especially in its reference to his treatment of his
characters: "He had dared to lift his characters up above the
average meanness of mankind, to let them live by their pro-
founder impulses."

Unfortunately, people in Asheville, his family included,
did not see the novel in the same light. Depending upon the
extent to which their lives had been exploited, individuals in
Asheville reacted violently. Tom had, admittedly, written
with "a naked intensity," making full use of all he had experienced. People were sure that they recognized themselves
and, worse, that other people could recognize them. They
were indignant at this invasion of their privacy.

Tom, while admitting that the book was "autobiographical," flatly denied that it was reportorial or that he had written with any malicious intent. What he had written of Asheville could just as easily have been written of Boise, Idaho.

But as the days passed, and more people read the book, the

bitterness increased in intensity. Mabel found that her friends were as icy to her as if she herself had written the book. She was snubbed by the members of the exclusive clubs in which she had established herself over the years. Now, just as she was coming to be accepted, the book threatened her position in the community.

People could talk of nothing else. It became a popular topic of conversation: people whispered about the appearance of so-and-so in the book, as though Tom had written a gossip column. He resented the implications that he had merely reported what he had seen and heard. At one point, he suggested that his Asheville critics should stand on the street corners, listen to all the gossip, take notes on what they heard, and see if the result would be a novel.

To Mabel, Tom wrote of his surprise and frustration: "I get cards and letters and phone calls from Asheville people from time to time. No one has been more surprised by the effect my book has had on some people than I have. I live in my own world: I go about looking, seeing, studying, observing, but the world I create is my own." This idea, in varying form, he repeated again and again. "I did not write about Asheville," he kept saying, "I wrote about wonderful, magnificent people, living in a world I made."

He was amazed that the people in Asheville were unaware of the book's impact beyond the mountains. "Doesn't it mean anything to the people at home to know that honest and intelligent critics all over the country have thought my book was a fine and moving one? Surely there are people there who are fair and generous enough to see that I am trying to become an artist," he protested to Mabel.

To the suggestions that he had written a malicious, gossipy, key-hole view of Asheville life, he cried, "Does anyone seriously think that a man is going to sweat blood, lose flesh, go cold and dirty, work all night and live in a sweatshop garret for almost two years, as I did, if his sole purpose is to say something mean about Smith and Jones and Brown?"

What really hurt and baffled Tom, though, was not the reaction of Asheville's ordinary citizens. The real hurt came from those extraordinary people whose opinions he valued and whose love and respect he wanted. Among these, of course, was Margaret Roberts, whose friendship and guidance had sustained him through most of his life. It was she who had first seen the golden talent he possessed. It was she who had cared for his mind and his spirit. More than anyone else in Asheville, it was she who had led him toward this moment when his creation would be offered to the world.

But Mrs. Roberts was shattered by Tom's portrayal of her husband—and herself. She wrote a sad and angry letter. Tom, in reply, tried to tell her that the bitterness in *Look Homeward, Angel* was not directed toward any one person, but against "the fundamental structure of life . . . which . . . seems cruel and wastefully tragic." He tried to reassure her about his methods: "Experience comes into me from all points and is digested and absorbed into me until it becomes a part of me . . . the world I create is always inside me, never outside me."

Tom tried by every means at his disposal to reveal to her the integrity of his book and the innocence of his intentions. But the wound was too deep to be healed with words. It was not until about three years before his death that there was any contact between Thomas Wolfe and the "mother of his spirit."

But, if he was depressed and at times enraged by the local reaction to his book, he was delighted with the reaction of the world at large. He received numerous letters, many of them from strangers. Mark Schorer, the author, wrote to him only a week after the book was published. Sinclair Lewis wrote about the greatness and power of *Look Homeward, Angel*.

Hugh Walpole, in a newspaper interview, referred to its nearness to perfection. Aline Bernstein and her friends all thought of Tom as the new young lion of American letters.

By the end of 1929, Tom had decided that he could no longer teach. Scribners had arranged for a large advance against the royalties from his next book. The royalties for *Look Homeward, Angel* would not start coming in until six months after its publication date. To enable him to begin work on the second novel, Scribners would give him an advance against its royalties, payable in monthly installments.

Simultaneously, Tom applied for a grant from the Guggenheim Foundation. In his application, he described his projected second novel, which was to be called *The October Fair*. "It tries to find out why Americans are a nomad race," he stated. "Why they are touched by a powerful and obscure homesickness wherever they go. . . . Why thousands of young men, like this writer, have prowled over Europe looking for a door, a happy land, a home, seeking something they have lost, perhaps racial and forgotten."

On Christmas Eve, Tom, lonely, wrote to Maxwell Perkins:

"One year ago, I had little hope for my work and I did not know you. What has happened since may seem a modest success to many people, but to me it is touched with strangeness and wonder: it is a miracle.

"You are now mixed with my book in such a way that I can never separate the two of you . . . I can no longer think clearly of the time I wrote it, but rather of the time when you first talked to me about it and when you worked upon it. You are one of the rocks to which my life is anchored."

With the Guggenheim grant and the money from Scribners, Tom was free to go to Europe again. This time, he would go without aid from his mother. And this time he would go as a promising young writer, a man to watch.

He felt secure about *Look Homeward, Angel*. He had experienced the feel of fame, the headiness of praise, the devastation of ridicule, the loneliness of misunderstanding. He knew that he had countless books to write; *The October Fair* was already shaping itself inside him.

Perhaps the most important thing he had gained was the "rock"—Max Perkins. Here was a friend, a strong figure, a source of hope and encouragement. With a swift and certain knowledge, Tom saw Maxwell Perkins as a strange, strong soul meeting his own.

He could not have dreamed, now, that the publication of *The October Fair* was four years in the future; that month after month of incredible, enervating work lay ahead; that fame would turn to ashes. He did know, however, that whatever glory lay ahead, it would be shared by Maxwell Perkins.

14

He was united to no image save that image which he himself created. He was bolstered by no knowledge save that which he gathered for himself out of his own life.

You Can't Go Home Again

IT WAS THE MIDDLE OF May, 1930, when Tom finally stood on the deck of the huge liner and watched Manhattan fading westward. He felt a momentary calm settling upon his spirit. For the next few days, the soft roll of the ship, the cool sea-wind, the bird-creak of wood and rope, would soothe him as nothing else could.

His mouth was painfully tender from recent oral surgery, his nerves razor-honed by the strain of it. His spirit was tender from the abuse he had received from Asheville. He had come to realize, though, that he had squandered his time—had spent it as though he had an inexhaustible supply of it—in worry about local criticism of the book.

He had wasted time, too, with the adulation. The sudden fame had been too great a temptation; he had attended too many parties, written too many letters, granted too many interviews.

Perhaps the most significant aspect of this trip, though, was that it brought to a conclusion his friendship with Aline Bernstein. They had quarrelled with increasing frequency and intensity. He had tried to avoid seeing her; and, when he did see her, they both tried to avoid the fights which had come to characterize their relationship. But, no matter how hard they tried, almost every meeting ended with anger, shouting, and tears.

Now this trip to Europe would provide the opportunity for a final break. He would not write to her, and he would keep his address a secret so that she would not be able to write to him.

So, as the great ship pushed its way across the Atlantic, Tom looked upon the trip as a new beginning.

His efforts to keep his whereabouts a secret failed. He had been in Paris only two weeks when some of Aline's friends found him. He fled to Rouen, and, when he returned to Paris early in June, he redoubled his efforts to conceal his address. Feeling rootless and terribly alone as he always did in Paris, he began outlining the new book and scrawling long pages of notes.

He worked four or five hours each day. But in spite of the most intense effort, he was unable to achieve coherence or unity. All he could get down on paper was an assortment of notes, ideas, lists. There was nothing which resembled unified and purposeful construction.

Late in June, Tom met F. Scott Fitzgerald, whose books also had been published by Scribners. Maxwell Perkins had thought it would be good for Tom to meet Fitzgerald and had urged Fitzgerald to look him up.

Tom's reaction to Fitzgerald, however, was not at all what Perkins had anticipated. Fitzgerald's notoriety repelled Tom almost immediately. His brittle sophistication, his air of boredom, his fondness for the wealthy and for the intellectual expatriates—all this was repugnant to Tom.

He immediately became defensive. Fitzgerald, as spokesman for the jazz age, made Tom feel clumsy, loud, boorish. In short, in Fitzgerald's presence, Thomas Wolfe felt like a hillbilly, just as he had in the 47 Workshop at Harvard.

Fitzgerald, of course, was unaware of this effect on Tom. He wrote to Perkins, telling him of his respect for Tom as a writer and as a person.

151

Under different circumstances, Tom might have been more generous in his attitude toward Scott Fitzgerald. Years later, when Fitzgerald had been victimized by unscrupulous newspaper reporters, Tom's attitude was sympathetic. But now he was experiencing too many difficulties to be very charitable.

His problems with his writing were making him irritable and suspicious. Tom frequently sought something outside himself to serve as a scapegoat for his inadequacies. In this case, it was Fitzgerald. Tom convinced himself that Fitzgerald, frustrated in his own work and jealous of Tom's success, was deliberately trying to interfere with his work on the second book.

In mid-July, Tom went to Switzerland. The compulsion to write was almost unbearable. "It seemed," he later wrote, "that I had inside me, swelling and gathering all the time, a huge black cloud and that this cloud was loaded with electricity . . . with a kind of hurricane violence that could not be held in check much longer . . . that this great black storm cloud had opened up and amid flashes of lightning was pouring from its depth a torrential and ungovernable flood."

Gradually, a theme developed in his writing. He stated it as "of wandering forever, and the earth again." He became absorbed in the operation of two great forces, working in opposition to one another yet ceaselessly and irresistibly drawn together. One of these forces was the one which drives men to wander, to search, to move to and fro across the earth in search of a father, hating their aloneness even while they covet it. Opposed to this force was the attraction of the earth, love, place, home.

He was struggling with this theme, trying to apply it to the mass of almost incoherent material he was producing. At the same time, he was trying to avoid the strong autobiographical overtones for which *Look Homeward, Angel* had been criticized. Yet, the material was becoming increasingly the Story of Thomas Wolfe, just as *Look Homeward, Angel* had been.

Tom's problem was not a lack of inventiveness which made autobiography necessary. Part of the problem was that he could not resist mining the rich ore of his own experience. Another significant contribution to the problem was that of his increasing tendency to identify himself with all American experience.

As he worked, alone in Europe, his loneliness and home-sickness brought forth an intense swarm of memories of America: its trains at night, its buildings, the colors and lights and beauty of everything he had seen and heard and felt in America. As this material poured into his notes and ultimately into his finished novels, they appeared as a recounting of his own intensely personal experience.

Tom also brooded a great deal about Aline. He knew that the break with her had been both necessary and right. Yet, it was a step he had taken with great heaviness of heart, remembering clearly Margaret Roberts' warning that the affair could have no end but in misery. Now, in Europe and alone, he recognized it as truth. Yet, while continuing the relationship would have brought nothing but pain, ending it had been equally painful. He carefully avoided contact with anyone who might reveal to her his whereabouts. When he began receiving letters from her, he went to Geneva, telling only Perkins and his English publisher where he had gone.

In England *Look Homeward, Angel* had been published in early July and the reviews, while not enthusiastic, were generally favorable. Shortly after he had gotten settled in Geneva, however, two caustic reviews of the English edition plunged him into a deep depression. Always sensitive to reviews, he was shocked by the venom of these two.

He described the reception of the English edition as "a catastrophe." To John Hall Wheelock, he wrote, "Some of the reviews have said things that I shall never be able to forget: dirty, unfair, distorted, full of mockery. . . . My book caused hate and rancor at home, venom and malice among literary tricksters in New York, mockery and abuse over here. Life is not worth the pounding I have taken. But if there is some other life, and I am sure there is, I am going to find it."

He wrote to Maxwell Perkins, a brief formal note which had the tone of a letter of resignation. He told Perkins that he was not going to write any more and that he would like to have sent to him any money which had accumulated in his royalties account.

He flew to Lyons and Marseilles, then to Arles and Provence. This was his first experience with air travel. He had always loved trains—the pounding of their wheels, the wail of their whistles, the luxury of their Pullman berths in which his great frame was never quite comfortable. But the airplane was exciting in a different way. In spite of the anger and gloom, he was cheered by the view of Europe below him as well as by the exhilaration of flight itself.

After a trip to the Black Forest, he went to London, where his English editor, A. S. Frere-Reeves, had leased an apartment for him. He was calmed by "the homely familiarity of English life and the sense of order and repose such a life can give one." Tom's sense of order and repose was considerably different from that of the English, however. He slept until mid-day. Then he walked, prowling the city he loved. He returned to the apartment around midnight and as the city slipped silently into sleep, he began to work. He would brew strong coffee, open his ledgers and begin to write. He drank the coffee, paced the floor, smoked countless cigarettes. He worked until the day's first light came, until he heard the sound of the milkman's horse turning into the dawn-empty street. Then he would fall exhausted into bed.

In this way he worked until, for the first time, he began to

see a clear figure emerging from his writing. "The work began to take on lineaments of design," he wrote. "These lineaments were still confused and broken . . . but now I really
did get the sense at last that I was working on a great block
of marble, shaping a figure which no one but its maker could
yet define . . ."

He kept to his hard schedule throughout the winter, possessed by the book. In February, 1931, he sailed for home convinced that he could finish the book in six months. He was
still unaware of the enormous complexity of the work, still
oblivious to the long labor that lay ahead.

Two external pressures bore heavily upon him once he was
back in the United States. One was the knowledge that he
must sooner or later meet Aline again. Now that he was back,
living in Brooklyn, it was inevitable that they would meet.
The dread of this accidental encounter lay like a dark shadow
on his mind.

A second source of concern was his family. When the stock
market crashed in 1929, Tom was too much involved in *Look
Homeward, Angel* to sense the tremendous impact it would
have on American life. It was months before he was very
much aware of the Great Depression. Of course, he knew that
the stock market had collapsed, and he knew that the country
was in a state of serious economic decline. But he knew these
things only academically, without any sense of personal in-
volvement.

But one day while he was still in Europe, he had read a very
brief newspaper account of the economic disaster in Asheville.
The people in Asheville had already experienced much difficulty as a result of the land speculations. Before they could
recover, the depression came, and the Asheville banks closed.
Depositors were destroyed. Even the municipal government
fell apart under the sudden economic strain.

Tom had immediately written home. He had also asked

155

Perkins to send money to his family. If he had no money in his royalties account, he hoped Perkins would arrange for an advance.

Now, back in Brooklyn, Tom saw the effects of the depression. He saw poverty as he had never seen it before. He saw the lines of men standing in despair before employment offices, waiting for the job that was not available. There were lines of men waiting in shame for the charity of a bowl of soup. He saw the homeless ones huddling for warmth in corners, alleys, and doorways. Everywhere he saw the hollow eyes, the bony, unshaven jaw, the uncut hair, scuffed shoes, the shuffling, apologetic walk of the hopeless and unemployed. At the same time, he saw the unmistakable signs of wealth: small rich islands in the swamp of poverty.

It would be a long time before such sights developed in him a significant degree of social consciousness. Now, when he saw these pathetic men and women, he merely turned away saddened and went back to his apartment to plunge into his work again.

He made little effort to organize, plan, or control his work at this stage. In a speech given almost four years later, he said, "The great job now was just to dig it up and get it down— somehow to record it, transform it into the objective record of manuscript . . . thousands and thousands of pages that would never be printed, that no reader would ever see . . . but at any rate would now be upon the record."

As Tom withdrew from Aline, he grew closer to Perkins. This relationship had been that of two men engaged in a singular task—never before had there been an editor like Perkins. Never before had there been a writer like Wolfe. And they were working in a unique literary situation. The "novel" that Tom was trying to "get down" was not just one novel. He was, without knowing it, writing huge chunks of many books:

From Death to Morning, Of Time and the River, The Hills Beyond, The Web and the Rock, and *You Can't Go Home Again.*

And their relationship was growing, changing both in nature and intensity. Tom had begun to look upon Perkins as a father; and Perkins, who had five daughters, came to accept Tom as a son. Tom began to go to Perkins with all his personal problems. And Perkins always had time for him. At the end of Perkins' working day, Tom would appear at the Scribner Building, and the two of them would go to the Chatham Bar, only three blocks away.

Perkins was obviously interested in Tom as a person, but he was unable to separate the person from the writer. Perkins had an extraordinary respect for talent along with a genuine willingness to help authors in direct ratio to the extent that they needed help. Tom needed it more than most.

Meanwhile, the legend of Thomas Wolfe was growing. His size, his willingness to talk, his constant night-prowling through the city, all made good newspaper copy. He wrote to Perkins about this. ". . . I resent any effort to present me as a cheap and sensational person. In spite of my size, appetite, appearance, staying up all night . . . I am not a cheap and sensational person. If there is going to be any publicity, why can't it tell the truth—that I work hard and live decently and quietly . . ."

As he worked on what continued to be a shapeless mass of material, he began to question his ability. ". . . I have all this material," he told Perkins, "but I have not the same hope and confidence. I have, on the contrary, a strong feeling of self-doubt and mistrust." He thought one of the factors which was destroying his self-discipline was the public reaction to *Look Homeward, Angel.* Success, he thought, might have hurt him: "I cannot work in the glare."

157

But the weeks dragged by, and he did work, stubbornly and blindly. Before he knew it, two years had passed since the publication of *Look Homeward, Angel*. And still he was far from producing the second book for which the critics were waiting.

15

———————•———————

The man who hopes to create anything in this world of enduring value must be willing to wreak it out of his spirit at the cost of unbelievable pain and labor.

Letter to George McCoy

EARLY IN 1932, Mrs. Wolfe came to visit Tom and he took great pleasure in showing her New York. They wandered about the city, Tom's huge, powerful figure exaggerated by his mother's diminutive stature. She was curious and interested in all her son showed her, but she was awed by none of it. "Julia E. Wolfe of The Old Kentucky Home," as she called herself, felt equal to anything the world might offer.

During Mrs. Wolfe's visit, and probably as a direct result of it, Tom developed an idea for a story. The story began with a woman telling a single, isolated incident, from which there was spun out a complex narrative spanning three generations. Tom called the story "The Web of Earth," and it was his intention to enter it in a contest that had been announced by *Scribner's Magazine*.

He began to work on "The Web of Earth" with confidence. Max Perkins was excited about it and had high hopes for it. Yet, as so frequently happened, both of them misjudged the time its completion would require. As the deadline for entries approached, Max became more and more nervous. Finally, just before the contest closed, Perkins entered "A Portrait of Bascom Hawke" in Tom's behalf.

When "A Portrait of Bascom Hawke" was published in *Scribner's Magazine* a short time later, Tom was engulfed in a storm of angry protest. His cousins felt that the story was in fact a portrait of Henry Westall and Mrs. Westall. It was, they insisted, not only an invasion of privacy and an act of cruelty and ingratitude but it was also an unflattering and degrading portrait, holding their parents up to ridicule.

Tom denied the accusations and defended himself as best he could against his cousins' wrath. Later it was announced that "A Portrait of Bascom Hawke" had tied for first prize. This brought Tom an unexpected $2,500.00, which was some consolation for the trouble the story had caused.

As spring approached, it became obvious that *The October Fair* could not possibly be published as a single novel. At one point, Tom mentioned his belief that it would require perhaps eight books. To one correspondent, he referred to it as "a series of novels . . . each complete in itself but all related to a single thing."

Tom, therefore, began to concentrate his efforts on completing what he had thought of as the first section of *The October Fair*. He had originally called this section "The Fast Express," but now as he began to see it as a separate novel, he changed the title to *K-19*. This was the number of the Pullman car on the fast train between Asheville and New York—the coach Tom always rode on his trips to and from New York. Since most of this section was already written, Tom was sure he could finish it in a very short time. Accordingly, Scribners announced that *K-19*, the new novel by Thomas Wolfe, would be published in the fall.

Tom delivered the 200,000 word manuscript to Max Perkins early in the summer. Perkins began reading it with joy and anticipation, and finished it in despair. Like Tom's entire concept of *The October Fair*, *K-19* sprawled. There was little unity, there were too many details, too many by-ways from the central core, and the whole thing was far too long. As gently as he could, Max told Tom that *K-19* was not publishable.

Tom's knowledge that Perkins was right did little to soften

the blow. But he hurled himself back into work again. Parts of *K-19* later appeared as scenes and episodes in *You Can't Go Home Again*, *Of Time and the River*, and *The Web and the Rock*.

By this time, almost four years had passed since the appearance of *Look Homeward, Angel*. Tom had driven himself ruthlessly. He had, he thought, written over a half-million words. Yet there was nothing that could even be called the outline of a novel. He had completely lost control of his material—if, indeed, he had ever had control of it at all.

Perkins, for his part, was confused. He had seen only parts of the manuscript, and, therefore, had only a splintered view of the work. Perkins was the finest editor of his time, yet he had never before worked with a writer like Wolfe. After some thought, he finally did evolve a simple and obvious plan. Tom was advised to begin the new manuscript at the point at which *Look Homeward, Angel* ended.

By spring, Tom had delivered almost 450,000 words of manuscript and Perkins joyfully anticipated completion by the end of the summer. There would be an enormous amount of cutting, and Perkins was aware of the violence of Tom's reaction to cutting. But the material was good, and Max came to believe that the new book would be decidedly superior to *Look Homeward, Angel*.

Yet Tom continued to write, adding scene after scene to the already too-long manuscript. Perkins saw the spring warm into summer, and still the end of the writing was not in sight. For weeks, he was awed by the continued outpouring. Then awe became fright: the novel was out of control again.

Perkins was also worried about Tom. The brutal way he was driving himself was cause for concern. His emotional and physical condition were deteriorating rapidly under the strain. The wide shoulders slumped with fatigue. Great circles appeared under the dark, haunted eyes. The eyes themselves came to be those of some wild creature. It became increasingly difficult for him to sleep, and, even when he slept, he was tormented by nightmares. He would wake from them, wet with the sweat of fear. He would get out of bed, drink vile coffee, smoke one cigarette after another, and work the remainder of the night.

In the fall, Tom got away from the work for a few days. He had visited several times in the Connecticut home of Robert and Marguerite Raynolds. Raynolds, a successful novelist, had written a favorable review of *Look Homeward, Angel* for *Scribner's Magazine*. "The review was the first I read of my book," Tom later wrote in a letter to Raynolds. "Max Perkins . . . read it to me over the phone and then I went out and walked about the streets in a great many different directions. I hope I may have that feeling of jubilation and glory many times hereafter . . ."

Raynolds had made a point of meeting Tom, and the two tall men became friends. Over a period of time, they had seen one another often with Raynolds going into New York or Tom visiting the Connecticut farm. Tom liked the Raynolds' children. He liked the calm house, the restful atmosphere. He once told Mrs. Raynolds that she should find a nice girl for him so he could marry and settle into the good life.

Now he and Robert Raynolds planned a trip into the Vermont mountains. Robert had known that Tom had been working too hard, but he was not prepared for the toll the book had taken on his friend's health. When Tom arrived, his cheeks were sunken, his face gray with fatigue, his eyes staring wide with exhaustion. Raynolds noticed that Tom spent most of the evening sprawled in a chair; he was too tired for his usual pacing back and forth when he talked.

The next morning, Tom and Raynolds climbed into Raynolds' car and left to the accompaniment of shouts from the children and excited barking from the dog. Since Tom had never learned to drive, he served as navigator. He pored over the map, reading aloud distances, the names of towns, rivers and mountains.

They stayed overnight in farmhouses. They ate enormous meals, hiked, and climbed mountains. At Middlebury, Tom noticed that his white shirt was "all used up." They finally found a store which had a shirt big enough for him: a red-and-black plaid, flannel shirt similar to the one Raynolds was wearing. Tom was very proud of the shirt.

Gradually, Tom recovered his energy. The cool fresh air, the long walks, the change of pace, the wholesome food, and the presence of his tall, quiet friend were all good for him. He returned to the city refreshed. He moved into a new apartment in Brooklyn and started work again.

He took another rest of a sort in January, 1933. He went with his mother to see the inauguration of Franklin D. Roosevelt. The election of Roosevelt had restored some of the nation's confidence and Tom's along with it.

Mrs. Wolfe was too small to see over the heads of the people who lined the sidewalk to watch the parade. Tom managed to get a chair for her to stand on, and he stood behind her, his big hands steadying her. He later said that all he saw was his mother's shoulders. But he was in fact delighted that she had seen the affair and had enjoyed it so much.

The year moved inexorably into spring, and Perkins felt at last that Tom had the novel "in the palm of his hand." But it was, at best, a shapeless thing. Tom was doing nothing to improve the book, except in terms of length. This was hardly an improvement, since it was already too long. But he wrote furiously all summer, isolating himself in his apartment and taking only an occasional period of rest. Perkins came to believe, with much justification, that Tom would never finish the book.

In the early fall, Perkins began considering the unheard-of

step of taking the book away from the author. Such a course of action violated basic principles of the author-editor relationship and placed far too much responsibility on the editor. Perkins spent weeks in indecision and uncertainty. Finally, in December, 1933, he quietly told Tom that whether he knew it or not, the book was finished.

An astonished Tom protested that the book was far from finished. He needed a few more months. But Perkins knew that when those months were gone, Tom would want a few more, then again a few more. And the book would grow beyond publishable length. Therefore, he insisted that Tom arrange all his manuscript into proper sequence and deliver it to him in two weeks.

When he had received the manuscript and had read it, he divided it into two sections. One section retained the title *The October Fair* and the other was called *Of Time and the River*. The second section was selected for first publication.

Of Time and the River was too long; so large sections had to be cut out. What would remain needed shaping and rearranging. Simultaneously, much new material would be required. One of the immediate difficulties was that Tom started over-writing the new material faster than Perkins could help him delete. So, even at the stage of cutting, the manuscript continued to grow.

Perkins and Tom threw themselves into a harsh regimen of work. At the end of the office day, Tom would go to Perkins' small office. They would cut, shape, develop ideas. They would talk over the work Tom had done since the previous day. After two or three hours' work, they would go to the Chatham for dinner and lay out the work that Tom would do before their conference the next day. Max had moved into the city, and, frequently, the two of them would work at his house until quite late in the evening.

This work required more effort than most men would have

been willing to give it. But Max Perkins' devotion to Tom's genuis drove him almost as furiously as it drove Tom. He was certain that Tom's talent was the greatest of the time. Later, on several occasions, he said that his work with Thomas Wolfe was the most meaningful and remarkable experience of his life.

His friends, however, viewed with dismay the work he was forcing himself to do. Several of them commented on the extent to which he was noticeably aging under the strain of his work with Tom.

In addition to the work itself, their relationship imposed a severe strain on both men. Both were obstinate, both were talented, both were dedicated to the production of a novel superior to *Look Homeward, Angel*. But Tom resisted even those cuts which he knew to be necessary. Since he felt that the book was still not finished, he resented the rewriting and new writing which would not have been necessary had he been allowed to finish it.

Both men were exhausted. Tom's resentment grew in proportion to Perkins' insistence that the work be done. With increasing frequency, Tom's volatile temper exploded, and there were harsh and angry words. Always, however, Perkins' calm stubbornness and cool intelligence prevailed. They worked through the spring and summer with resentment just under the fragile surface of their relationship.

In the early fall, Tom went away for a few days' rest. When he returned, he was shocked to learn that the publication of *Of Time and the River* had been announced for the spring of 1935. The manuscript had been sent to the typesetters, and proofs were beginning to arrive.

Tom was baffled and angry. The book, he insisted, was still unfinished. Perkins had rushed into print with a far-less-than-perfect piece of work. The book, he was certain, would be poorly received, and it would be Perkins' fault. Yet the public, unaware of what had happened, would naturally criticize the author.

But as publication date approached, Tom's anger and resentment cooled. He forgot the bitterness and accusations and remembered only the selfless work his friend had poured into the book. He began to write a long statement as a sort of preface, in which he acknowledged his debt to Max Perkins.

Perkins might have been touched by this gesture. But he was also likely to have been opposed to it. Tom had so often accused him of ruining the book that lavish praise now would be insincere.

Most important, however, was that Tom's proposed preface seemed to say that he could not have written the book without Perkins. Tom had written in some detail of the nature of the work they had done, and the critics were almost certain to say that Perkins' role had exceeded that of an editor.

Tom was persuaded to shorten the dedication. When the book appeared in March, 1935, the dedication was

TO

MAXWELL EVARTS PERKINS

A great editor and a brave and honest man who stuck to the writer of this book through times of bitter hopelessness and doubt and would not let him give in to his own despair, a work to be known as *Of Time and the River* is dedicated with the hope that all of it may be in some way worthy of the loyal devotion and patient care which a dauntless and unshaken friend has given to each part of it, and without which none of it could have been written.

167

The idea that none of the book could have been written without Perkins would be reiterated and reinforced in a little book called *The Story of a Novel*. Tom had no idea that this belief—that Perkins was indispensable—would form a violent vortex down which would disappear one of the finest friendships in American literature.

16

Now I had an overwhelming sense of shame greater than any I had felt before. I felt as if I had ruinously exposed myself as a pitiable fool who had no talent and who once and for all had completely vindicated the critics who had felt the first book was just a flash in the pan.

The Story of a Novel

Tom's over-reaction to life in general was intensified by publication dates. The appearance of *Look Homeward, Angel* had been a soul-wrenching experience for him. In the six years since then, he had agonized over the publication of every story he had written. And now he was fearful of the reaction to *Of Time and the River*. His fears were increased by his certainty that the book was unfinished and had been prematurely published.

He and Perkins were in agreement that Tom should, by any means possible, avoid the stress of publication day. He, therefore, sailed for Europe and was in Paris on March 8, 1935, when the book was released in New York.

In Paris that day, he strode about the city alone, worried, ashamed of what he was sure was a literary disaster. That night, he paced back and forth in his room for awhile, then spent the rest of the night stalking through the dark streets.

After three days of this self-torture, he forced himself to go to the American Express office for the cablegram which he knew Perkins had sent on publication day.

The cable from Perkins assured him that the reviews were magnificent. They were critical in some of the ways both of the men had anticipated. But, in general, they were highly favorable.

Tom felt tension seeping out of him. He stuffed the cable

into his pocket and went out to find something to eat—his first meal in three days. He reread the message several times before he decided that Perkins was trying to be kind and was, therefore, being cruel. As darkness settled along the Seine, Tom began to feel that the book was as bad as he had originally thought and that Perkins was trying to hold back the bad news. His depression deepened for two more days.

Finally, desperate, he cabled Max: ". . . you are the best friend I have. I can face blunt truth better than the damnable incertitude. Give me the straight plain truth."

Perkins immediately cabled back that all the reviews were comparing *Of Time and the River* to the work of the greatest writers. The book was, Perkins assured him, being spoken of as a truly great book.

One of the earliest reviews appeared in the *Saturday Review of Literature*. Henry Seidel Canby, the reviewer, had criticized the "unfinished" quality of the book and had pointed out Tom's failure to achieve his purpose. But he thought the book was ". . . one of the most American books of our time. It is in the direct tradition of those earlier anguished spirits and great seekers on our soil, Thoreau, Melville and Whitman."

On March 10, the New York *Times* had printed a review by Peter Munro Jack. "No American novelist," he wrote, "is so vigilant in the perception of character or so urgent in its expression. Nor is anyone, except perhaps Dreiser, so unafraid of the immensity of life. This tremendous capacity for living and writing lifts *Of Time and the River* into the class of great books. It is a triumphant demonstration that Thomas Wolfe has the stamina to produce a magnificent epic of American life."

On the same day, Burton Rascoe's review appeared in the *Herald-Tribune*. "Thomas Wolfe has a magnificent malady," Rascoe wrote. "It may be called gigantism of the soul. And . . . because he is so lyrically and vociferously articulate, we have a voice in this novel which sounds as if it were from demons, gods and seraphim in chorus . . ."

Not all the reviews were favorable. Not all the favorable reviews were totally favorable. But the book was well-received. It quickly climbed the best seller lists. Within a few weeks after publication, it had sold 20,000 copies.

Tom spent a few restless weeks in England after leaving Paris. Then he decided to go to Germany. A regulation of the German government made it impossible for his royalties on the German edition of *Look Homeward, Angel* to be taken out of the country. The logical thing for Tom to do was to live in Germany until his royalties account was exhausted.

The German edition of *Look Homeward, Angel* had been a great success and Thomas Wolfe was more highly regarded in Germany than in the United States. The American reception of *Of Time and the River* was already known in Germany. His German publishers were planning to bring the book out there as soon as possible. They were therefore delighted to have him visit Germany, and saw to it that his arrival was heralded by newspapers and radio. He saw his book and his photographs in bookstore windows. There were pictures of him and articles about him in all the newspapers and magazines.

He was suddenly famous. His publishers arranged a series of parties which caught the attention of the press. Martha Dodd, daughter of the United States Ambassador to Germany, asked him to be the guest of honor at a party at the Embassy. Miss Dodd had admired *Look Homeward, Angel* and now Tom visited her frequently at the Embassy. The two became good friends.

Martha Dodd tried to tell Tom something of the sinister rise of Hitler. But Tom was too busy enjoying Germany and his own fame to take Hitler seriously. Never a student of politics, he could not yet grasp the terrible implications of

Nazism. In this blindness, he certainly was not alone: most people of the thirties were unconcerned about Hitler.

Tom saw the brown-shirted marchers, heard the tramp of German boots, saw the swastikas everywhere. But it seemed to him the play of children. It was several years before he saw that these children were playing a deadly game in deadly earnest.

Now, he attended parties, read the newspaper stories about himself, ate the good, heavy food, and walked the lovely streets of Berlin.

In a very real way, fame caught up with Thomas Wolfe that spring in Germany. He had clearly established himself as a major novelist. *Of Time and the River* had great flaws in it—Tom was more aware of this than the critics were. Yet it was a brilliant piece of work, and was generally recognized as a great novel.

It was with enthusiasm that Tom travelled about Germany, and it was with excitement and childlike eagerness that he returned to New York.

Tom's boat docked on July 4, 1935. He had stood on deck, gazing long at the New York skyline, brilliant and magic in the summer morning sun. Waiting for him there were a number of newspapermen: fame had come to him in the United States as well as in Germany. He talked with the reporters for a while. Then he saw Max Perkins sitting on a luggage truck.

Perkins seemed upset, but insisted that nothing was wrong. They got Tom through customs, then went to a riverside restaurant for dinner. In the restaurant, Tom was again aware of a troubled expression on Perkins' face, a nagging note of preoccupation in his voice. He insisted that Perkins tell him what the matter was.

Max told him. Aline Bernstein had made a point of telling him that she would do everything in her power to prevent the

173

publication of *The October Fair* if she appeared as a character in it, which of course she did. To Perkins, this was a serious threat which could destroy all the work Tom had done.

Tom was not at all disturbed by this, and soon had convinced Max that there was nothing to worry about. By the time they had finished their lunch, Perkins was once again in a happy frame of mind. The gloom was gone; the two friends were laughing and remembering and anticipating.

They spent the remainder of the afternoon walking from one favorite place to another. Tom stalked along with his great, lumbering strides, his shaggy head held high, his arms swinging, his dark eyes bright with excitement. Perkins, shoulder-high to Tom, matched his stride, joyous in Tom's joy as a father rejoices in the happiness of a son.

They went to many places, including the attic where Tom had written most of *Look Homeward, Angel*. They brought the day to a close atop a tall building from which they could look down upon the lights of the city below and around them. Years later, this would be the subject of Tom's last letter.

Now, neither man knew how little time was left to them. Tom, at that moment, was a great writer, with dozens of books yet to be written. He had approached the high point of his creative power and he knew it and there was nothing in his heart but joy and certainty.

17

———————•———————

His mind was ablaze with a stream of swarming images,
stamping a thousand brilliant pictures on his brain with
the speed of light, the flare of a soaring rocket.

The Web and the Rock

PERKINS WAS EAGER TO PUBLISH a collection of Tom's stories. The collection was to be called *From Death to Morning*, and there were many decisions to be made. The stories needed to be arranged in proper sequence. There would be proofs to be read. And timing was important if they were to have full advantage of the popularity of *Of Time and the River*.

Tom, however, was unwilling to give much attention to all these details. The reviews of *Of Time and the River* had been clipped and saved for him. He spent a great deal of time reading them, laughing triumphantly over the favorable ones and muttering about the few which were unfavorable. Even more delightful to him than the reviews were the letters he had received. There were letters of unqualified praise from major writers of the time. There were letters of congratulations from old friends and acquaintances, many of whom he had not seen for years.

The letters which pleased him most, however, were from very ordinary people whom he had never met. These strangers had read the book, and something reached out to touch them, and they wrote to tell him of it. It was such letters that he appreciated most.

One letter which was to have far-reaching effects came

from the University of Colorado, asking Tom to participate in its writers' conference to be held in the summer. Tom readily agreed: it would be a worthwhile experience for him and it would provide him an opportunity to see a part of the country he had not yet visited.

His responsibilities at the conference would be threefold. He would talk with individual writers, read their manuscripts and offer whatever criticism and assistance he could. Second, he would participate with other writers in a series of panel discussions. And he would deliver one formal lecture.

As a basis for this lecture, he decided to use the notes for the long dedicatory preface he had written for *Of Time and the River*. This expanded version of the preface would later be serialized in *Saturday Review of Literature* and would be published as a small book with the title *The Story of a Novel*.

He spent some time working on the lecture, answering his mail and doing a little work on *From Death to Morning*. He and Max resumed their schedule of daily meetings in the late afternoon.

By the end of July, Tom was in Boulder for the two weeks' conference. It was a rewarding experience. His lecture was an outstanding success, and he enjoyed thoroughly his participation in the panel discussions. He was stimulated by his contacts with the aspiring young writers from whose work he found several manuscripts which he thought good enough to recommend sending them along to Perkins.

Perkins had expected Tom to return to New York at the close of the conference in order to finish the work on *From Death to Morning*. Instead, Tom went to California. He had been overwhelmed by the Rockies, and the wanderer in him would not let him rest until he had crossed them. In Santa Fe, he met Edna Ferber, with whom he was impressed. He went on to Hollywood where he met the famous motion picture people of the time, including Jean Harlow.

177

He was adamant about the publication of *From Death to Morning*. "You must not put the manuscript of a book of stories in final form until after my return to New York," he wrote to Max. "If that means the book of stories will have to be deferred till next spring, then they will have to be deferred. I will not consent this time to allow the book to be taken away from me and published until I myself have had time to look at the proofs . . . I really mean this, Max."

He was not concerned about taking advantage of the publicity resulting from *Of Time and the River*. The very idea of it seemed somehow dishonorably commercial. He outlined the three major problems to which he would give attention. First, he thought, he should settle the suit Madeleine Boyd, his former agent, had brought against him for the collection of allegedly unpaid agent's commissions. Second, he had to do a "thorough, honest and satisfactory job" on *From Death to Morning*. Finally, he had to finish *The October Fair*. Failure in any one of these, he wrote, would result in "another shameful . . . waste of talent at the time of its greatest fertility."

For the first time, Tom felt capable of telling Maxwell Perkins what he would and would not do. His conviction that *Of Time and the River* had been hastily published made him anxious to avoid any further carelessness. Paradoxically, it was the outstanding success of that "unfinished" book which made it possible for Tom to assert himself so forcefully.

When he finally began his return trip to New York in mid-September, Tom stopped in St. Louis to see the house his family had lived in when he was a child—the house in which Grover had died.

The names of the streets had been changed, and the neighborhood was much different. When he found the house, it too had changed: the fence and the carriage house had been torn down, and nothing about the house was as big as Tom had remembered it. Yet, it was unmistakably the one he had lived in years before. Tom later wrote of this visit in a story called "The Lost Boy," published in *The Hills Beyond*.

When he finally arrived in New York, he refused to go to work until he had found an apartment with a view of the river. He finally found one with a fine view, with the added attraction of being only a short walk from Perkins' house. It was in this apartment that Tom had a custom-built bed in which, for the first time in his adult life, he could stretch his body out to its full length.

He got settled into this apartment and flung himself into the job of reading printers' proofs for *From Death to Morning*. The book was published in November, and the reviews ranged from indifferent to sharply critical. Though this was a depressing time, Tom bore the criticism better than most of his friends would have anticipated.

As usual, he was having trouble getting to work again. Neither he nor Max felt any great enthusiasm for *The October Fair*. Part of their difficulty was the fear that Aline Bernstein would bring suit against them. And part of it was simply inertia. Tom was also making notes for a proposed book about night in America which he was tentatively calling *The Hound of Darkness*. This was never finished, but parts of it later appeared in two novels and in an article published in *Vogue* in 1938.

Another idea which was demanding his attention was a novel about "a good man abroad in the world . . . who sets out in life with his own vision of what life is going to be . . . what he is going to find, and then the story of what he really finds." This projected novel he called *The Vision of Spangler's Paul*.

He also polished and perfected the lecture he had given at the writers' conference at the University of Colorado. It finally appeared in *Saturday Review of Literature* in three installments in December, 1935.

From the moment he had first heard of this piece, when it was still in the form of a preface to a novel, Max had opposed its publication. Yet, it was such a remarkable record of an author's experience that he was not unaware of its value. His fear that its publication would be harmful never completely left him, but it faded. This fear was based on his belief that the piece gave him more credit than was good for Tom to admit. There would be those, he was sure, who would say that, by his own admission, Tom was less an artist than his editor.

After it had appeared in *Saturday Review of Literature*, Max consented to its publication as a book. *The Story of a Novel* was published in the spring of 1936.

Immediately afterwards, there began a series of quarrels between Tom and Max, sparked primarily by a slashing review of *The Story of a Novel*, but brought on, too, by the impossibility of their complicated relationship.

It was inevitable that Thomas Wolfe and Maxwell Perkins would quarrel seriously. Their personalities were too complex, and their lives touched at too many sensitive points. They were good friends, they were father and son, they were hero and hero worshipper, they were editor and author. The many roles in which these two men found themselves were intolerable for any length of time.

Also, there was, in the darkness of Tom's soul, need for someone greater than himself, to whom he could anchor his life. And the same demon demanded the destruction of his own idols. The process of destruction had begun for Perkins; the first strains had already been placed upon the friendship.

Then came the publication of *Of Time and the River*. Perkins' unprecedented step of taking the novel away from him gnawed at Tom. He dealt with this episode at some length and without anger in *The Story of a Novel*. Yet, he continued to harass Max about it, writing letters accusing him of betraying his best friend, of ruining his novel, of wasting his talent.

Then, there were arguments and misunderstandings over Tom's royalties. Tom intimated that Scribners' had, with Perkins' knowledge, misled him even if they had not forthrightly cheated him. This unfounded charge was a direct result of Tom's lack of knowledge of, or real interest in, the details of the publishing business.

A further aggravation resulted from a complex libel suit which had been brought against him in the spring of 1936. He was already involved in two other suits, a defendant in one, plaintiff in the other. Attorneys' fees and judgments wiped out his royalties account. His reaction was one of outrage, and much of his anger was directed against Max.

Another festering spot was the material which Tom was beginning to write about a publishing company: Scribner's. Tom felt that Perkins had no right to interfere. Perkins had thought it was all right for Tom to write about his family and his friends in Asheville. Now, Tom reasoned, it should be all right to write about friends in New York.

Perkins was distressed, however, because much of what Tom knew about the firm he had learned directly or indirectly from him. At least, that is what people would think. Perkins, to whom honor was a way of life, would have inadvertently contributed to the betrayal of his friends and colleagues.

Max knew that Thomas Wolfe would write what he had to write, even if it meant that Perkins would have to resign. Tom could not take the resignation threat seriously: he knew that Charles Scribner would never accept the resignation of the finest editor in the business.

Tom and Max were drifting apart, too, in their view of the world. It was this, and only this, that Tom referred to as a factor in the fictional version of their separation at the close of *You Can't Go Home Again*. For years, Tom had no political views. He was so involved in digging into his own life that he

181

paid little attention to the social, political, and economic world in which he lived.

He had always thought of himself as a socialist. As the depression deepened, his social awareness grew and, with it, his liberalism. As he saw brutalizing poverty alongside ostentatious wealth, he began to question the values he had always accepted. Gradually, he began to think of himself as a "liberal" and of Perkins as a "conservative." Actually, neither man could be so neatly classified.

The difficulty came when Tom wanted to include some of his shiny new political and economic philosophy in his novels. When Perkins objected, Tom accused him of trying to "censor" his writings. Perkins' objections were not to Tom's political and economic ideas. He objected, and strenuously, to Tom's superimposing them upon characters which they did not fit. It was a matter of literary craftsmanship, not philosophy.

Thus, by the spring of 1936, their friendship had been subjected to severe strains. Yet, each man prized the other's friendship, and each tried to save it.

The Story of a Novel was the burden under which the friendship began to crumble. This little book has great value as the record of how one of the world's fine novels came to be written. It is an articulate statement of one artist's painful development. But at the time of its publication, it was a personal catastrophe for Tom.

Shortly after it appeared on the market, the *Saturday Review of Literature*, which had originally published it as a serial, carried a review of it by Bernard De Voto. The title of De Voto's article was "Genius is not Enough." The first few paragraphs were devoted to reviewing *The Story of a Novel*. The remainder was a caustic appraisal of Wolfe's talent in general.

It was De Voto's contention that Wolfe might well be a

genius. But even a genius ought to know how to do something; in Tom's case, he ought to know how to write, which, he insinuated, Tom did not.

Tom read the review with shame and horror. It was a stinging, slashing article, written to hurt. Tom writhed as he read references to his ". . . whirling discharges of words . . . unrelated to the proper business of fiction" and to "raw globs of emotion, aimless and meaningless jabber, claptrap, belches, grunts, and Tarzan-like screams."

He was shocked that De Voto would state in print that he was unable to decide whether Thomas Wolfe was an incompetent writer or a mental case. *Look Homeward, Angel*, De Voto wrote, "looked like one of two things, there is no telling which. It looked like the self-consciously literary posturings of a novelist too young and too naive to have learned his craft. Or from another point of view, it looked like a document in psychic disintegration."

Finally, De Voto appeared to decide that Thomas Wolfe was both unbalanced and incompetent: "Mr. Wolfe is still astonishingly immature . . . and has mastered neither the psychic material out of which a novel is made nor the technique of writing fiction."

In the long run, Tom would have recovered from the shame and hurt and anger caused by paragraph after paragraph of this sort of malice. The permanent devastation was wrought by De Voto's statement that the one essential characteristic of the artist "has existed not in Mr. Wolfe but in Maxwell Perkins." De Voto believed that all the organizational ability and critical judgment writing a book requires came "not from the artist's feeling for form and esthetic integrity, but from the offices of Charles Scribner's Sons."

De Voto summed it up by saying that the important question was whether Wolfe could, in his next book, manage to master his material. If so, he said, "he must do so inside himself: Mr. Perkins and the assembly line at Scribners can do nothing to help him."

These stinging insults meant only one thing: Tom would have to find another publisher. The De Voto article left him no choice. He could not possibly have another book published by Scribners after this statement that it was their assembly line, presided over by Perkins, which supplied the judgment and the essential craftsmanship of which a book is made. Thomas Wolfe would have to find another publisher in order to prove to the world that he could write without Maxwell Perkins.

Tom did not face this issue immediately. He complained about all the other problems—the royalties, the lawsuits, the differing ideologies—and said little about the credit given by De Voto to the Scribner "assembly-line." His anger and resentment about the article were directed primarily against De Voto's use of a review of a relatively minor book as a vehicle from which to attack everything else Wolfe had written.

Fortunately, Tom could go to Europe again at this point. The German edition of *Of Time and the River* had been well-received, and his royalties account there had built up again. And, again, he would have to spend the money in Germany.

Also, a German steamship line had offered to give him free passage in exchange for some articles to be published in a magazine distributed by the company.

Tom was delighted to be back in Berlin again. He renewed his acquaintance with Martha Dodd, and the two of them spent many hours together, dining, walking down the broad streets and through the lovely parks.

Berlin was the site that year of the Olympics and Tom attended faithfully. He had always been interested in athletics, and he enjoyed the games immensely.

But this was a new and militant Germany. Even Tom could

184

see the effects of the Nazi regime. Everywhere, he saw the great red and white banners with the ominous black swastikas. Everywhere, he saw the uniforms and the stern faces of Hitler's youth, and heard the steady tramp of German boots. Most of all, he saw the effects of repression: the uncertain and covert glances, the lowered voices, the flicker of fear across his friends' faces, the little ghosts of distrust and suspicion.

To Perkins, he sent a postcard showing marching soldiers with the message: "We can never learn to march like these boys—and it looks as if they're about ready to go again."

In a long letter to his friend Jonathan Daniels, he wrote of his fear that the German virtues of "devotion and self-sacrifice have been given over to a misdirected purpose, a false ideal." He described Europe as "a volcano of poisonous and constricted hatred which threatens to erupt at any moment."

Although he had these grave misgivings about Germany, he fell in love with a German artist, Thea Voelcker. But their courtship was a stormy one. After many quarrels, they parted company, never to see each other again.

Tom came away from Germany, a country he once had called his own, thoroughly convinced of the evils of Nazism. He was aware that any public statements of criticism of Germany would harm the sales of his books there. Yet he had no doubt about what he must do. First, he wrote to the steamship company, telling them that he could not write the articles he had promised them and enclosing a check for his passage to relieve himself of the obligation to write articles favorable to Germany. Then, for a magazine in the United States, he wrote his impressions of what he had seen and heard in Germany. Called "I Have a Thing to Tell You," this article resulted in the banning of his books in Germany. It was later included in *You Can't Go Home Again.*

Tom had been back in New York less than twenty-four hours when he started quarrelling with Max Perkins, who had been critical of some of the material Tom had submitted. Tom's reaction was angry and resentful. Perkins rejected the material, simply because it was poorly-written. Tom insisted that he had not liked it because it was about Scribners. Day after day, thereafter, they argued about it.

Simultaneously, Tom was enraged about the lawsuit in which he was involved. A family had sued him for libel, seeking damages of $125,000.00. Tom's contract with Scribners absolved the firm of all responsibility for libel. They were under no obligation to consider themselves in any way responsible.

The firm volunteered, however, to pay half the costs and judgment, provided Tom would be cooperative with them and their attorneys, to which he readily agreed.

Tom was astonished when the publishers' attorney urged an out-of-court settlement. The affair dragged on and on, with everybody but Tom eager to settle the case without going to court. Tom wanted to fight it out in the courtroom because he thought this would discourage any others who might be thinking of suing him. Finally, the case was settled out of court for approximately $3,000.00, of which Tom's share was less than $1,500.00.

This was a fortunate settlement, but Tom was not happy with it: he considered the whole affair a cowardly compromise of principle. He was working steadily now on *The Vision of Spangler's Paul*, but he still had time for bitter reflection and constant accusations against Scribners and Perkins.

He refused to stop by Perkins' office in the afternoons, but he was still a frequent visitor in his home. In fact, he spent Christmas Day there, before his departure for New Orleans where he spent New Year's.

In New Orleans, there was a constant round of parties for

him. He drank too much, rested too little, and wrote to Perkins almost constantly. Many of the letters, however, were never mailed.

In these letters, he was almost sentimental: "Even if we have come to the end of our publishing connection . . . for God's sake, let us try to save our belief and faith in one another . . ."

Sometimes, he was accusatory: "Are you—the man I trusted and reverenced above all else in the world—trying . . . to destroy me?"

Sometimes, he was self-pitying: "I am broke, I have lost everything, I do not think I can go on . . ."

At least once, he was insulting: "I cannot bear to see you just a good but timid man."

Max bore all this abuse with remarkable patience. His attitude was that of a father toward a wayward son: he might be hurt, he might become momentarily angry, but he would never totally reject Tom.

Knowing that nothing he could say would really change Tom's attitude, he nevertheless explained his position patiently and clearly. He denied Tom's accusations firmly and without rancor even though he knew that the dark spider of suspicion now sat at the center of the web of Tom's life. Tom had convinced himself that Perkins was either a cruel man trying to destroy him or a cowardly man permitting others to do it.

In spite of Tom's harsh accusations, unjust charges, and unfounded suspicions, Max remained unchanged. For nine years he had been Tom's "dauntless and unshaken friend." He would not now permit himself to become less than that.

On his way back to New York, Tom stopped at Chapel Hill. He had not been in North Carolina since the publication of *Look Homeward, Angel*. It was a pleasure for him to see again

Carolina's red, red earth, rolling hills, tobacco fields and tall pines. It was good to hear again the slow, soft Carolina speech.

He marvelled at the changes which had occurred on the campus and revelled in the friendly welcome given him by the faculty and students. His old friend, Jonathan Daniels, gave a dinner for him in Raleigh. Then Tom went to Warrenton as a guest of William Polk, whom he had known as a student both at the University of North Carolina and at Harvard.

In New York, he resumed his work on *The Vision of Spangler's Paul*. He was heartened by the extent to which his agent, Elizabeth Nowell, had been able to place his stories in magazines. Miss Nowell had for many years worked for Scribners and Tom was one of her first clients when she left the firm to establish her own literary agency. His stories continued to appear in *Scribner's Magazine*, but she had also sold stories to *Yale Review*, *New Yorker*, *American Mercury*, *Harper's Bazaar*, *Saturday Evening Post*, and *Redbook*.

In the spring, Tom had an opportunity to play a role he always enjoyed but seldom indulged in: that of host. Jonathan Daniels and his wife came to New York, and Tom eagerly arranged a small dinner party at a well-known restaurant. He had always liked and admired Daniels, and now he was pleased to have him as a guest in New York.

The party included the Perkins, and the evening began beautifully. Tom was happier than he had been for months, and Max was pleased to see him so relaxed. Tom was eager to see that everybody had a good time, and there was much happy talk and laughter.

Then someone inadvertently mentioned the "Genius is not Enough" article by Bernard De Voto.

Tom grew silent.

The conversation passed quickly over the painful subject, and the conversation swept around the suddenly-sullen host.

Of all the people present, only Max Perkins was aware of the awful effect the careless remark would have on Tom. He watched Tom's face and saw the anger creeping across it.

In a short while, Tom was insulting everybody at the table. He began to drink, and his voice rose as he became increasingly angry. Soon, people at nearby tables were looking at him.

Finally, Max tried to calm him with a gentle remonstrance. Tom turned on him in a blind fury, threatening to hit him. Max was undoubtedly shocked by this threat from his huge friend, but, if he was frightened, his fear did not show. When Tom actually tried to hit Max, he was restrained by Daniels and another guest.

While Tom's anger blazed, Max looked up at him with eyes in which there was no trace of fear. Whatever Max might have been, he was not the weak and timid man Tom had come to think he was.

In that moment, Tom must have felt that, for all his great bulk, he was not as big a man as Maxwell Perkins.

18

Something has spoken to me in the night, burning the tapers of the waning year; something has spoken in the night and told me I shall die, I know not where.

You Can't Go Home Again

By April of 1937, Tom felt in need of a vacation. He decided to combine it with a trip to Asheville where his mother was deeply engrossed in legal problems of her own. Throughout the Florida and Asheville land booms as well as the depression which followed, Mrs. Wolfe's financial affairs were a confused tangle, so that even she was at times uncertain of her financial stability. Now, in the spring of 1937, she learned that she owed a large sum of money to an Asheville bank. The bank brought suit against her and her heirs.

Tom had already experienced more than his share of lawsuits. He immediately had himself eliminated as an heir. In so doing, he forfeited any share he might have had in his mother's estate. But he also avoided any consequences of the bank's lawsuit.

Though he was no longer directly involved in his mother's financial difficulties, he wanted very much to help her in any way possible. It was after some hesitation that he decided to go to Asheville.

This was not a decision made lightly. At the time of the publication of *Look Homeward, Angel* there had been several threats against his life if he ever returned to Asheville. Partly for that reason, he had refused to return. He was now certain that, with the passage of so many years, the physical danger was practically nonexistent. But he knew that he would receive an icy reception: in the Carolina mountains, people have long memories.

His trip south was a leisurely one. Perhaps unconsciously he wanted to delay his arrival in Asheville as long as possible. On May 8, he was in Burnsville, not far from Asheville. Late in the evening, he went into a soda shop for a soft drink. Two men, one of whom was named Phil, were standing on the sidewalk in front of the shop, talking. When Tom came out of the shop some time later, they had been joined by a third man, who was arguing with Phil.

Suddenly this man and Phil were fighting. Bystanders quickly separated them, then fled for cover when Phil suddenly drew a gun from his pocket. There was a frantic dash for shelter of any kind—Tom leaped behind a car parked at the curb.

Four times the spring night was shattered by the roar of the gun, and the man lay twisted in the street. Tom was shaken by this street killing: a few years before it could have happened to him had he returned to Asheville. Tom talked with the police when they arrived and was told that he would be subpoenaed as a witness when Phil came to trial.

The next day, Tom arrived in Asheville, nervous and anxious. To his astonishment, he was welcomed as an unofficial favorite son. Dozens of people came to the Old Kentucky Home to see the hometown boy who had become famous. The house rocked with loud talk and laughter as the boisterous Wolfes enjoyed the limelight focused on their brother.

People of the town gave parties in Tom's honor. He spoke to civic clubs and was interviewed by the newspaper reporters. Most important of all, he saw Mr. and Mrs. Roberts again. Although the friendship could never again be what it had been before the publication of *Look Homeward, Angel*, at least it was partially restored.

193

Tom was so pleased with the welcome he had received in Asheville that he foolishly decided to stay. He rented a comfortable cottage several miles outside the city, where he expected to be able to write in peace and quiet. But there was almost too much peace and quiet. Tom needed to see people, especially at night. He was unable to sit in solitude hour after hour. And to add to the disadvantages of the location, since he had never learned to drive, he was dependent on family and friends for transportation. There was also the problem of food. He had anticipated having someone to cook for him, but help wouldn't stay with him very long. Therefore, although he hated cooking for himself, he was forced to do so.

Of course, he could always go into Asheville for an occasional meal. But this involved him in the volatility of his family. Frank, with whom all the family quarrelled, was living in Asheville. Mabel and Ralph Wheaton had recently moved there. Fred was a frequent visitor, and Effie came occasionally.

When all the Wolfes were together, there was always noise and confusion. There were sudden explosions of temper followed by clumsy apologies. And there was always a sort of abrasion of the spirit; so that Tom found any prolonged contact with his family caused an emotional strain which interfered with his work. His mountain idyll ended with the summer: he returned to restful New York!

While he was still in Asheville, however, he had attempted to establish contact with a publisher to replace Scribners. To his surprise, changing publishers was not as simple as he had thought it would be.

Some publishers were reluctant to talk with him because they were not certain that he had really broken with Scribners. Some might have been unwilling to negotiate because they had guessed, correctly, that Maxwell Perkins was unaware of Tom's search for a new publisher. Finally, some firms were afraid of Tom: they knew of his temperament, and they were aware of and unwilling to accept for themselves Maxwell Perkins' long ordeal with Thomas Wolfe.

One man who was not afraid was Edward Aswell, an editor for Harper and Brothers. Ironically, it was Bernard De Voto who told Aswell that Wolfe had left Scribners. Aswell was quick to establish contact with Elizabeth Nowell, Tom's agent. In November, after Tom returned to New York, with no authorization from Harpers, he offered Wolfe a $10,000.00 advance against royalties for *The October Fair*. This was an astonishingly good offer, yet Tom delayed signing the contract until the middle of December. There had, in the meantime, been other offers, but, after much delay and indecision, he chose to work with Harper and Brothers.

He spent Christmas in Aswell's home, and the two men became better acquainted. They began working on Tom's book shortly after the first of the year. Tom had lost interest in *The October Fair* partly because of the long delay in publishing it. He was reluctant to start work on it again. Aswell, however, showed him how *The October Fair* could be re-written as a part of *The Vision of Spangler's Paul*.

Tom immediately began to work with enthusiasm. Gradually, he began to abandon the two titles and started referring to the new book as *The Web and the Rock*. It finally appeared as two separate novels, *The Web and the Rock* and *You Can't Go Home Again*.

Characteristically, Tom's vision lashed him into a frenzy of work. His efforts renewed his vision of the country, his dreams of time and of the strangeness of life here in America. He set a murderous pace for himself, slipping quickly into his familiar schedule which worked so well for him but which took such a devastating toll of his energy. He had been working on the two books long enough to have accumulated great sheaves of manuscript. And now, as he began working again, the stacks of paper grew higher and higher.

Gradually, everything fell into proper sequence. By the middle of May, 1938, he was able to turn the manuscript over to Edward Aswell. And what a manuscript it was! Aswell later reported that in a single stack it came up to his chest. It consisted of over four thousand typed pages—about one and one-quarter million words.

With the completion of the manuscript, Tom was free to accept an invitation to speak at a literary dinner at Purdue University. The fee would provide enough money for him to take a trip to the Pacific Northwest, the only part of the United States he had not seen.

As usual, he was elated at the prospect of crossing new rivers, seeing new mountains, meeting new people. Also, as usual, he left New York in a roar of confusion, almost missing his train.

His appearance at Purdue was a great success. His address was similar to the one he had given at the University of Colorado Writers' Conference. It was, however, characterized by considerably more candor, a certain light-heartedness and marvelous humor. He reviewed the circumstances of his life which had made him a writer, poked fun at some of the things he had written in college, and talked about his objectives and his methods. Both Tom and the audience thoroughly enjoyed the evening.

He stayed at Purdue two days, then went to Chicago for the weekend. He lumbered through the city's streets, gazed long at Lake Michigan, and went to a famous German restaurant for the heavy food he enjoyed so much.

From Chicago, he went to Denver to visit friends he had made at the Colorado writers' conference. He had planned to stay there two or three days, but the welcome from his friends was so warm that he stayed a week. It was not until the middle of June that he arrived in Portland.

Without taking any time to rest, Tom began a two-week

tour of the western national parks as a guest of a newspaperman and an automobile association official. They left Portland on a bright June morning. Tom had a small ledger in which he immediately began to scribble his impressions of all that he saw. This journal was later published as *A Western Journey*.

They drove southward across Oregon and down the length of California to Yosemite and Sequoia National Parks. They crossed the Mojave Desert into Arizona, where their route swung back northward to the Grand Canyon. In Utah, Tom saw Bryce Canyon, Zion National Park, and the Salt Lake country. They went into Idaho and Wyoming to see the Tetons and Yellowstone. They went as far north as Peace Park on the Canadian border of Montana, then headed west toward Spokane, Grand Coulee, Mt. Ranier National Park, and Seattle.

Tom was always raised to a high pitch by travel and this trip was especially exciting. Tom had always been obsessed with the wonder of America and the great vistas of the west were especially impressive. The great brooding mountains and deep canyons, huge lakes and geysers, broad sweeps of lonely land and lonely sky—everything here was built on heroic proportions, and Thomas Wolfe loved life on the grand scale.

When the trip ended in Seattle, Tom was exhausted. But before he could give in to his fatigue, he received a telegram from Edward Aswell. Aswell had finished the manuscript and thought it was magnificent. In Aswell's opinion, the manuscript contained some of the finest writing Tom had ever done, and he was sure the critics would look upon the book as the greatest thing he had ever written.

The exhaustion vanished and his spirit soared again. He decided that it would be appropriate in a reverse sort of way to celebrate Independence Day on British soil. Therefore, on the

197

spur of the moment, he caught a boat to Vancouver, British Columbia.

He arrived in Vancouver feeling ill. He checked into a hotel and promptly crawled into bed. As the day progressed, his temperature rose and chills began. The holiday was turning into a miserable misadventure, and he decided to return to Seattle right away.

It was several hours before the next train to Seattle, and Tom simply could not bear the thought of spending those hours in a hotel room. He, therefore, wandered around the city, tiring himself still more. Finally, in a state of utter exhaustion, he boarded the train.

He managed to get some sleep, clutching his arms tight across his chest in an attempt to squeeze away the pain which was beginning to glow white-hot in his lungs.

In Seattle, Tom went directly to a hotel, secured a room, and fell gratefully into bed. His cough was worse and the pain in his chest was almost unbearable. His temperature was not yet dangerously high, but it left him weak and very uncomfortable. For several days, he remained alone, his needs supplied by sympathetic hotel employees.

When his condition did not improve, he telephoned his friend James Stevens who came at once to see him. Stevens realized immediately that Tom should not remain alone in a hotel room. After some argument, he persuaded Tom to submit to medical attention and quickly arranged for his admission to Firlawns Sanitarium about ten miles outside the city.

The physician, Dr. E. C. Ruge, diagnosed Tom's illness as pneumonia, but he strongly suspected tuberculosis. He immediately sent a telegram to Edward Aswell who in turn contacted Mrs. Wolfe and Fred.

Ralph Wheaton had been ill for some time, and it was impossible for Mabel to leave him on such short notice. Fred went to Asheville, where it was decided that he should go at once to Seattle. Mabel would go later if it developed that she was needed.

Within a few days, Fred was in Seattle. The first thing he did was to talk with Dr. Ruge. He learned enough about Tom's illness to realize that his recovery would be very slow. Then, in the afternoon, he saw Tom. Dr. Ruge had already told Tom that Fred was coming to Seattle.

"They sent for you, didn't they?" Tom said to Fred. "They told you I was very sick and that you should come."

"Not exactly, Tom," Fred answered carefully. "They did tell me you've been ill. But the fact is, I've had only one vacation in five years. Now I'm taking a full month off to see this part of the country."

To all outward purposes, Tom accepted Fred's explanation, but he had a growing certainty that he was seriously ill. Fred quickly came to the same conclusion. He went out to Firlawns every day to visit Tom, and, with each visit, he was more convinced that Tom should be in a larger hospital.

About a week after Fred arrived in Seattle, Tom was moved to Providence Hospital. There his chest was x-rayed, and there was clearly a visible irregularity on his right lung. Both the x-ray specialist and Dr. Ruge were convinced that this was a tubercular lesion. Other doctors were equally sure that it was only the result of the pneumonia.

Tom did not respond to treatment. His appetite did not diminish, yet he began to lose weight. Then the time came when it was necessary for Fred to return to his job in Spartanburg. Mabel arrived to relieve Fred of his responsibility for Tom's care. This was one more indication to Tom that his illness was a matter of real concern to his family.

Fred planned to leave the day after Mabel arrived. But, when visiting hours were over and he said goodbye to Tom, Tom said, "I'll see you in the morning, Fred."

Fred couldn't bear to disappoint his brother, and postponed

his departure for a day. The next night, before he could tell Tom that he was going home, Tom again said that he would see him in the morning. This happened night after night; Fred did not actually get away from Seattle until late August.

All this time, Tom was maintaining a steady low-grade temperature, along with headaches which gradually increased in intensity. Simultaneously, he was becoming frightened and increasingly aware of the dangerous nature of his illness.

"I'm sneaking this out against orders," he said in a letter to Maxwell Perkins. "But I've got this hunch and I want to write these words to you."

"I've made a long journey and been to a strange country and I've seen the dark man very close; and I don't think I was too much afraid of him, but so much of mortality still clings to me—I wanted most desperately to live, and still do, and I thought about you all a thousand times and wanted to see you all again . . ."

"Whatever happens—I had this 'hunch' and wanted to write you and tell you no matter what happens or has happened, I shall always think of you and feel about you the way it was that Fourth of July day three years ago when you met me at the boat and we went out to a cafe on the river and later went on top of the tall building and all the strangeness and the glory and the power of life and of the city was below."

Mabel was assured by the doctors that Tom could soon be released from the hospital. Tom was delighted with their use of the world "release" for he always hated hospitals, and this one was like a prison to him. Therefore, he felt it was a singularly appropriate word.

He was childlike in his happiness. Leaving the hospital was much more than a physical change: it was also the release of his spirit from its dark prison of fear.

He told Mabel to get an apartment for them, and recommended one in a building which had a view of Puget Sound. They would stay in the apartment for a few weeks, then go home in a leisurely fashion. He wanted to visit San Francisco on the way.

Mabel managed to get the apartment he wanted. It was beautifully furnished and had a view of the Sound. She had a large, old-fashioned, and very comfortable bed put in the living room for Tom. And since Tom's appetite had not diminished, she laid in a supply of food with the intention of preparing all of Tom's favorite dishes.

Mabel received a great deal of help from Annie Laurie Crawford. Annie Laurie had once been superintendent of nurses at the hospital in Asheville, and she was now taking special courses at the University of Washington Hospital. During Tom's illness, she had frequently cooked his favorite foods and brought them to him. Now she arranged her vacation in such a way as to be free to stay in the apartment with them and help Mabel care for Tom.

To Tom's great annoyance, the doctors delayed his release in order to do further x-rays. His headaches had grown worse, and he had begun to have difficulty in judging the sequence of events. It was almost unbelievable that Tom's vast and powerful memory, on which all his writing depended, had begun to fail. At times, for instance, he could not remember that Mabel had been in Seattle for days. He would frequently greet her as though she had just arrived.

The physicians finally agreed to dismiss Tom. But they warned Mabel sternly that the x-rays had revealed a brain condition, probably an abscess or tumor. They released Tom on a bright afternoon early in September, telling Mabel that she should take him at once to Johns Hopkins and place him under the care of Dr. Walter Dandy, one of the nation's leading brain specialists.

Tom walked out of the hospital wearing his favorite brown

suit and a battered felt hat. He was haggard and worn; he had lost fifty pounds and was very unsteady on his feet. But he was elated and joked happily about being "released."

At the apartment, he was pleased with the view and with the large vases of flowers many friends had sent. He was especially glad to see Annie Laurie cooking a southern meal for him.

That evening, Tom was visited by a physician who had been sent by Harper and Brothers. He examined Tom, asked about the headaches, checked his reflexes, and asked questions designed to test his mental alertness.

Then knowing that Tom needed it, he spoke very bluntly: Tom was seriously ill and should not be making plans to stay in Seattle. He should already be on his way to Baltimore. Sensing Mabel's inability to act decisively on this matter, he himself called Mrs. Wolfe and told her that Tom was on his way to Baltimore, seriously ill. She should meet Tom, Mabel, and Annie Laurie in the Chicago station. He then arranged for Tom's admission to Johns Hopkins and also made train reservations. The following night, Tom, Mabel, and Annie Laurie were on an eastbound train.

In Chicago, a railroad employee met the train with a wheelchair to take Tom to a first aid room where he could lie down until departure time for the Baltimore train. Mrs. Wolfe had brought Tom some fruit, and he was pleased to have it. He was in good spirits and teased his mother constantly.

By midnight, they were on the train to Baltimore. Tom's sleep was fitful, but Mabel fell into the deep sleep of exhaustion. Mrs. Wolfe and Annie Laurie were awake most of the night.

By the time they were putting Tom into the ambulance in Baltimore, Annie Laurie was on the crisp edge of hysteria.

She was spent, physically and emotionally, and had come to believe that Tom would never recover.

Observing this, Mabel called up her reserve energy. While her mother and Annie Laurie went with Tom in the ambulance, she took care of all their luggage, and arranged for rooms for them near the hospital.

That evening, Tom enjoyed a short visit with Edward Aswell. Aswell attempted to put Tom's mind at ease about the purpose of his visit. He had come to Baltimore, he said, to tell Tom about how wonderful his new book was going to be. They chatted for a while, with Tom occasionally losing touch with the subject of conversation. Finally, he drifted off to sleep.

Aswell talked with Dr. Dandy; then the two of them talked with Mabel. Mabel found it difficult to believe that Tom was as ill as the doctors insisted he was. The doctor therefore summed it up bluntly: if Tom had either cancer or tuberculosis of the brain, the case was hopeless. If he had a tumor, his chances of survival depended upon its location. At best, Tom's chances of living were about five out of one hundred.

Later, Dr. Dandy talked to Tom, explaining that he wanted to perform an operation to relieve the pressure and thus end the headaches. The operation would also facilitate the making of more x-rays.

The operation was performed and the x-rays were made. After studying them, Dr. Dandy scheduled Tom for surgery the following morning.

Meanwhile, Fred had arrived from Spartanburg, and his presence took a heavy burden off Mabel. Max Perkins also arrived. He knew that he would not be able to see Tom. But it was characteristic of him to be there, sturdy and strong should he be needed.

The surgery the following morning required three hours.

This little group—Mabel and Fred and their mother, Edward Aswell and Maxwell Perkins—waited together and alone. Finally Dr. Dandy and Annie Laurie came down the corridor.

"It's hopeless," Dr. Dandy's voice was blunt and flat. "He has miliary tuberculosis of the brain."

Tom regained partial consciousness that afternoon. One of the family was with him constantly that night and the following day and night. By Wednesday, they were exhausted, and were persuaded by the hospital staff to get some much needed rest. Tom was by this time in a coma.

During the long Wednesday night, he was attended constantly by physicians and nurses. The dark, past-midnight hours stalked slowly by. Then dawn came to the city and the huge hospital.

And, with the sun, death came to Thomas Wolfe, September 15, 1938.

Tom was buried near his father and his brothers, Grover and Ben, in the silent Carolina mountains. He had died only a few days before his thirty-eighth birthday. The news of his death spread throughout the land he had loved so much. All the newspaper stories in one way or another speculated on what his future might have been, had he lived.

Some authorities were sure that Tom would have "written himself out"—that he had said all he had to say. Others were certain that Tom was just at the beginning of his career and that death had ended a brilliant talent before it was fully developed. Still others felt that, with his slowly developing social conscience, Tom would have become the real spokesman for his generation.

To Maxwell Perkins, who knew Tom better than anyone else, such speculation was meaningless. This sensitive and knowing man wasted little thought on what might have been. He could think only of the magnitude of Wolfe's accomplishments during those nine brilliant and tormented years since the publication of *Look Homeward, Angel*.

Perhaps Maxwell Perkins, more than anyone else, understood the significance of the quotation from *The Web and the Rock* which is carved on the stone above Thomas Wolfe's grave:

DEATH BENT TO TOUCH HIS CHOSEN SON

WITH MERCY, LOVE AND PITY AND PUT

THE SEAL OF HONOR ON HIM WHEN HE DIED.

FOR ADDITIONAL READING

BOOKS BY THOMAS WOLFE

Look Homeward, Angel. New York, Charles Scribner's Sons, 1929.
The Web and the Rock. New York, Harper and Brothers, 1938.
Of Time and the River. New York, Charles Scribner's Sons, 1935.
You Can't Go Home Again. New York, Harper and Brothers, 1940.
From Death to Morning. New York, Charles Scribner's Sons, 1932.
The Hills Beyond. New York, Harper and Brothers, 1935.
A Western Journal. Pittsburgh, University of Pittsburgh Press, 1951.
The Story of a Novel. New York, Charles Scribner's Sons, 1936.
The Letters of Thomas Wolfe, edited by Elizabeth Nowell. New York, Charles Scribner's Sons, 1956.
Thomas Wolfe's Letters to his Mother, edited by John Skally Terry, New York, Charles Scribner's Sons, 1943.
Mannerhouse: A Play in a Prologue and Three Acts. New York, Harper and Brothers, 1948.

BOOKS ABOUT THOMAS WOLFE

Daniels, Jonathan *Thomas Wolfe: October Recollections.* Columbia, South Carolina, Bostick and Thornley, Publishers, 1961.
Johnson, Pamela H. *Hungry Gulliver.* New York, Charles Scribner's Sons, 1948.
Kennedy, Richard S. *The Window of Memory.* Chapel Hill, University of North Carolina Press, 1962.
McElderry, Bruce R. *Thomas Wolfe.* New York, Twayne Publishers, 1964.

Norwood, Hayden *The Marble Man's Wife: Thomas Wolfe's Mother*. New York, Charles Scribner's Sons, 1947.

Nowell, Elizabeth *Thomas Wolfe: A Biography*. Garden City, N.Y., Doubleday and Co., 1960.

Pollock, Thomas C. and Cargill, Oscar *Thomas Wolfe at Washington Square*. New York, New York University Press, 1954.

Raynolds, Robert *Thomas Wolfe: Memoir of a Friendship*. Austin, University of Texas Press, 1964.

Turnbull, Andrew *Thomas Wolfe*. New York, Charles Scribner's Sons, 1968.

Walser, Richard, ed. *The Enigma of Thomas Wolfe*. Cambridge, Harvard University Press, 1953.

Watkins, Floyd C. *Thomas Wolfe's Characters: Portraits from Life*. Norman, University of Oklahoma Press, 1957.

Wheaton, Mabel Wolfe and Blythe, Legette *Thomas Wolfe and His Family*. Garden City, New York, Doubleday and Co., 1961.

INDEX

209

effects of, 180
publication opposed by Perkins, 180
published, 180–181

"The Tar Heel" (newspaper)
Wolfe managing editor, 51
Wolfe writes for, 41, 43
"The Third Night" (play), 54

University of North Carolina, 36, 37,
55–56
University of Virginia, 31, 34

The Vision of Spangler's Paul (novel),
188, 195

Washington Square College, 80–81,
136
Watt, Homer Andrew, 77, 80, 96, 114
The Web and the Rock (novel), 157,
162
length, 195–196
epitaph from, 205
"The Web of Earth" (story), 160
"Welcome to Our City" (play), 73,
75, 76, 84
Westall, Henry, 61, 161
"A Western Journey" (journal), 197
Wheaton, Mabel Wolfe, 7, 27, 35, 60,
194
cares for father, 38
illness of, 95
marriage, 35
reaction to *Look Homeward, Angel*,
139, 145
Wheaton, Ralph, 35, 194
Wheelcok, John Hall, 137, 153
Williams, Horace, 52, 80
Wolfe, Benjamin Harrison, 7, 34, 42
and Fred, 21
and Wolfe, 20–21, 47–49
Asheville newspaper, 27, 58
health, 38
illness and death, 47–51
Wolfe, Effie, see Gambrell, Effie
Wolfe

Wolfe, Frank, 7, 65, 194
Wolfe, Fred W., 8, 49, 70–72, 95, 194,
203–204
and Ben, 21
graduate of Georgia Tech, 70
newspaper boy, 12
Norfolk, Virginia, 44–47
Seattle, Washington, 198–200
U.S. Navy, 38

Wolfe, Grover Cleveland, 7, 12, 14–16
Wolfe, Julia Elizabeth Westall, 37,
55, 72–73, 102
boarding houses, 9, 23–24
financial affairs, 118–119, 155, 192
frugality, 24, 27, 37, 48–49, 102
marriage, 7
St. Louis, 9
visits Wolfe in New York, 160
Wolfe's death, 202–204

Wolfe, Mabel, see Wheaton, Mabel
Wolfe

Wolfe, Thomas Clayton
and air travel, 154
and Ben, 20, 47–49
and Clara Paul, 39
and Grover, 17
and James Joyce, 110
and monument shop, 25
and Old Kentucky Home, 24
and public library, 25
and time, 42–43, 82
and trains, 13, 28
appearance and mannerisms, 8, 30,
36–37, 41, 82–83
as actor, 54
as college freshman, 36
as newspaper boy, 30–31
as playwright, 54–55, 62–63, 68, 74–
76, 106
as teacher, 81–84, 123
at Harvard University, 60–62
at North State Fitting School, 28–
29, 31–32
at Johns Hopkins, 203
at Orange Street (elementary)
School, 21–22

211